The Immortal Company

How to Lead Beyond Your Lifetime (Transitional leadership)

Victor Ariyibi

Dedication

To every founder who has dared to dream, who has carried the weight of a vision on their shoulders, and who has fought against the odds to bring that vision into reality, this book is for you. I know the labour, the sleepless nights, and the unseen sacrifices it takes to start something from nothing and to nurture it until it stands on solid ground. This is your story as much as mine.

To my beloved wife, Tolulope, my partner of over twenty years, thank you for standing by me through every season of building, every late night, every difficult decision. You have been my anchor, confidant, and constant reminder of why the journey matters. This book would not exist without your unwavering love and sacrifice.

To my three precious daughters, Simisola, Kanyinsola, and Oyindasola, you are my strength, joy, and pillars. Every day, you remind me of what legacy truly means. My love for you is beyond words, and I dedicate this book as much to your future as to my present.

To my father, whose quiet wisdom and resilience continue to inspire me, even when the road has not always been easy, thank you for teaching me the values that still guide me.

To my grandmother, of blessed memory, who raised me to believe in myself and gave me everything she had, even when she had so little, though you are no longer here, your love lives in me every day.

To my mother-in-law, gone too soon but never forgotten, we carry your memory in our hearts, with love and gratitude.

To my mentors, who have inspired me, corrected me, and believed in me, I am forever grateful for your guidance. To my friends who have walked this path with me, you know yourselves. Though I cannot name everyone here, please know that your impact on my life is deeply cherished.

Finally, to my teams, past and present, across every company I have founded and every venture I have led. To those who stood by me for years, even decades, through challenges and triumphs: this book is for you. It is for your dedication, loyalty, and belief that together, we can build something greater than ourselves. Keep dreaming for every entrepreneur who has started, stumbled, and started again. Keep building. It will all work out.

Forward

By Mason Grant, Director of Project Management, The Global Publishers

When Victor Ariyibi-Oke first approached me with the manuscript of *The Immortal Company*, I felt something I rarely experience in this industry: a sense of profound honour. As a publisher, I see countless books pass through my hands every year, manuscripts filled with ideas, ambitions, and sometimes even brilliance. But every so often, one work stands apart. It carries not just words, but a spirit. It contains not just arguments, but a calling. *The Immortal Company* is such a book.

What struck me most as I read was not simply Victor's sharp insight into why so many organisations collapse after their founders step aside, though that truth is powerful and painful. What moved me was the heart behind his message. Here is a man who has lived what he writes. He has built institutions, he has let go of them, he has seen them grow beyond him, and he has learned the lesson that so many founders never discover until it is too late: a company must be designed for continuity from its very first breath.

In boardrooms around the world, I've seen the tragic paradox play out: billion-dollar companies with endless cash flow vanish almost overnight, not because their products failed, not because the market rejected them, but because they never transitioned from a one-man dream into a living, breathing institution. They were never built to outlast the visionary at the top. Victor's work exposes this truth with honesty, but more importantly, he provides a roadmap out of it.

This book is not an abstract theory. It is not another volume of empty business jargon. *The Immortal Company* is a living testimony, sharpened by Victor's personal journey and crafted into a framework that every entrepreneur, CEO, and leader can apply. Within these pages, he urges us to take conscious, decisive steps: to build systems that survive personalities, to foster cultures that flourish without dependency, and to empower teams who can carry the torch long after we are gone.

If you are an aspiring entrepreneur, you will find in these pages a compass to guide your early steps. If you are already leading a business, you will find a mirror that challenges you to examine whether what you are building will endure. And if you are a seasoned executive, you will rediscover the responsibility of legacy, the sobering truth that leadership is not about how brightly we shine during our tenure, but how well we prepare the ground for those who will come after us.

I will tell you plainly: every CEO I know needs this book. Every board member I sit with should read it. Every founder who dares to dream of building something greater than themselves must wrestle with their message. Because this is not just a book about leadership or strategy; it is about immortality, not of the individual but of the vision, the values, and the institutions that shape the world.

Victor's central message is clear: lasting companies are never accidents. They are born from foresight, humility, and intentional design. To read this book is to be confronted with both a challenge and a gift. The challenge is to build differently, to lead with legacy in mind. The gift is the knowledge that it can be done, that you, too, can build something that will not die when you step away.

For me, writing this foreword is not just a professional duty. It is a personal privilege. Because I believe, with every fibre of conviction, that *The Immortal Company* is a book that will not just inform but transform, it is a work that will travel far beyond these pages, into boardrooms, classrooms, and family tables, wherever dreams of continuity and greatness are born.
So, read carefully, read slowly, and read with the knowledge that what you hold in your hands is more than a book; it is a call to action, a guide to legacy, and a map to immortality.

Mason Grant
Director Of Project Management
The Global Publishers

Part I: Understanding Transitional Leadership

1. **Introduction: Why Most Companies Die with Their Founders**
   - The founder's paradox: visionary strength vs. operational fragility.
   - Statistics on family businesses and founder-led companies that fail after succession.
   - Your personal journey: exits and lessons from businesses that lived beyond you.
2. **Defining Transitional Leadership**
   - What transitional leadership means in corporate governance.
   - Difference between temporary management, succession, and transformational leadership.
   - Transitional leadership as a bridge between founder-driven and institution-driven organisations.
3. **The Cost of Founder Dependency**
   - Why founder-centric leadership creates hidden risks.
   - Stories of companies that collapsed after founder exit.
   - Psychological and emotional barriers founders face in letting go.

Part II: Building for Continuity

4. **Laying the Foundation for an Organisation that Outlives You**
   - Vision vs. systems: institutionalizing culture and mission.
   - Structuring for scale: from "one-man business" to enduring company.

o Lessons from your personal exits and leadership
    transitions.

Part IV: Leading Beyond Yourself

11. Designing Organisations That Outlive the Founder

- Embedding values into systems, not individuals.
- Codifying culture and processes.
- Building an innovation engine to keep the company relevant.

12. From Founder to Statesman: Redefining Your Role

- Moving from operator to visionary.
- Becoming a board chair, advisor, or investor in your own
  company.
- Detaching ego from leadership.

13. Pitfalls to Avoid in Leadership Transitions

- Micromanagement and inability to let go.
- Poor board composition.
- Ignoring succession until it's too late.

Part V: The Legacy of Transitional Leadership

14. Building Institutions, Not Just Companies

- Shifting from wealth creation to legacy creation.
- Societal impact of companies that live beyond founders.
- Why lasting companies matter for communities, industries,
  and nations.

Introduction

WHY MOST COMPANIES DIE WITH THEIR FOUNDERS

In almost every part of the world, a silent tragedy keeps repeating itself in the business landscape: promising companies, some worth millions, others deeply loved by their communities, collapse the moment their founders step aside or pass away. It does not matter if these businesses once employed thousands of people, created wealth across generations, or stood as symbols of innovation. The pattern is hauntingly familiar: the founder leaves, and the organisation dies.

Why does this happen? Why is it that so many companies cannot seem to outlive the very individual who birthed them? Why do organisations, built on years of sweat, sacrifice, and brilliance, vanish into irrelevance once the founder's chair becomes empty?

The answer lies in a paradox at the heart of entrepreneurship: **the same vision, drive, and personal involvement that make a founder indispensable often make the company untransferable.**

The Founder's Paradox

Founders are, by nature, visionaries. They see opportunities others overlook. They are willing to take risks, work sleepless nights, and carry the burden of responsibilities no one else dares to shoulder. Their relentless drive and deep personal attachment to the company often become the fuel that powers its growth.

However, herein lies the paradox: while their presence builds the company, their dominance often prevents it from growing

1

organically.

Many founders unintentionally become so tightly woven into the fabric of the organisation that removing them unravels the entire system. The business strategy lives in their head. Key customer relationships depend solely on their handshake. The culture is a mirror of their personality. Decisions, whether minor or significant, pass through their desk. Ultimately, the company is not an institution; it is an extension of the founder.

And when the founder steps away, the "company" discovers it was never truly a company. It was a one-man or one-woman empire, now without its emperor.

The Data Doesn't Lie

Consider this: according to global studies, nearly **70% of family-owned businesses fail to survive into the second generation.** By the third generation, the survival rate falls to below **15%.** That means for every hundred companies founded with vision, grit, and determination, fewer than fifteen will still exist by the time the founder's grandchildren come of age.

Even among large corporations, the problem is evident. History is littered with examples of powerful companies that collapsed immediately after their founding leadership disappeared. Kodak, once a pioneer in photography, failed because its leadership was unable to transition into a new generation that embraced digital technology. BlackBerry, once the king of mobile devices, lost its footing because the founding leadership refused to loosen its grip and allow new thinking to guide the company into a smartphone-driven era.

The numbers and stories tell us one thing: the issue is not about size, industry, or geography. The problem is about **leadership transition.**

Why Founders Struggle with Letting Go

Transition is hard, not just for the company, but for the founder. For many founders, their identity is inextricably linked to their business. The company is not merely a project; it is their life's work, their proof to the world that they mattered. To imagine the company existing without them feels like imagining life moving on without their name being part of the conversation. This is a fundamental challenge faced by every business, from startups to established corporations.

This is why some founders resist creating structures that reduce their centrality. They insist on approving every decision and micromanage teams. They distrust anyone who dares to dream differently. Unknowingly, they build a culture of dependency where employees are trained to wait for instructions rather than think independently.

The result? The founder feels indispensable, and indeed, they are. But this is also the reason their exit equals the company's funeral.

Real-Life Examples of Founders Letting Go

The challenges of letting go are not unique. Many founders have faced this challenge, with some experiencing difficult outcomes.

Steve Jobs and Apple

While a visionary, Steve Jobs's initial departure from Apple in 1985 is a classic example of a founder's departure causing instability. After he was forced out, the company struggled to innovate and lost market share, illustrating the "cost of founder dependency." His return in 1997 was necessary to save the company, underscoring his integral role and highlighting the lack of a strong, independent institutional structure at the time.

George Zimmer and Men's Wearhouse

The founder of Men's Wearhouse, known for his iconic "I guarantee it" slogan, was fired in 2013 by the very board he helped create. Zimmer's struggle to cede control and his public disputes with the board showed his reluctance to accept a less central role in the company's direction. His exit, while not the "company's funeral," illustrated the intense personal and professional conflict that can arise when a founder's vision clashes with corporate governance.

Travis Kalanick and Uber

Kalanick's aggressive, founder-driven culture defined Uber in its early years but also led to numerous scandals and legal challenges. His eventual forced resignation in 2017 showed that a founder's personal identity and leadership style, while effective for a time, can become a liability to the institution's long-term sustainability and market reputation. This example underscores the importance of a smooth transition to an institution-driven leadership model.

From Business to Institution

There is a fundamental difference between a business and an institution.

- A **business** is dependent on the founder.
- An **institution** is built on systems, governance, and a culture that outlives any individual.

Founders build businesses. Transitional leaders build institutions.

When a business becomes an institution, its values, mission, and decision-making frameworks are no longer locked in the founder's brain. They are documented, codified, and practiced across the organisation. Leadership is no longer concentrated in a single person, but is distributed across boards, executives, and governance structures. Investors, advisors, and co-leaders provide stability. Leadership pipelines prepare the next generation.

This is why global corporations like IBM, General Electric, and Unilever outlive their founders by centuries. They evolved from being someone's dream into being institutions with transitional leadership at their core.

My Own Journey with Transitions

I have not reached this conclusion solely from reading books. I have lived it.

As a CEO, I have built companies that no longer require my presence. I have exited businesses that now operate without my daily involvement. In fact, I have experienced both the joy of seeing organisations thrive beyond me and the pain of realizing how close some were to collapse because of decisions I made as a founder.

It took me years to learn that authentic leadership is not about being indispensable. It is about creating an organisation that flourishes when you are absent. That is the mark of legacy.

The hard truth I discovered, and which this book is built upon, is this: **if your company cannot survive without you, then you never truly built a company. You constructed only a job for yourself.**

The Urgency of Transitional Leadership

In today's world, the need for transitional leadership has never been more urgent. **Globalisation**, rapid technological shifts, and the speed at which industries evolve mean that no single leader, no matter how brilliant, can guarantee the future of an

5

organisation.

Founders must accept that leadership is a temporary role. What matters is not how long you hold the reins, but whether the company can gallop forward once you let go.

Transitional leadership is the discipline, structure, and mindset that ensures companies survive these critical handovers, whether from founder to co-founders, from one CEO to another, or from one generation to the next. It is about building resilience, continuity, and governance into the organisation's DNA.

Why This Book Exists

This book exists because too many businesses die with their founders. It exists because I have seen firsthand how avoidable these deaths are. It exists because leaders deserve a roadmap for building organisations that outlive them.

Through this book, I will share principles, frameworks, and personal experiences that demonstrate how companies can effectively adopt transitional leadership. We will explore governance, succession planning, leadership pipelines, the role of investors and boards, and the practical realities of letting go.

By the time you finish this book, you will no longer see your company as your personal empire. You will see it as a living institution, designed to thrive beyond you, capable of surviving second and third generations, and strong enough to outlast time itself.

Because at the end of the day, **a true leader does not just build a company. A true leader builds continuity.**

Chapter 2
DEFINING TRANSITIONAL LEADERSHIP

When organisations reach a point of leadership change, whether through the founder stepping down, a CEO resigning, or a generational shift in ownership, they enter one of the most vulnerable phases of their existence. The direction taken in this period often determines whether the company flourishes into an enduring institution or collapses into memory. This is where **transitional leadership** becomes critical.

Transitional leadership is not just about finding a replacement for the leader. It is about creating the bridge between the **old and the new**, ensuring continuity while enabling necessary change. It requires a careful balance: preserving the company's essence while adapting it for the future.

What Transitional Leadership Means in Corporate Governance

In the context of corporate governance, transitional leadership is the structured approach to managing leadership change within an organisation. It emphasizes:

1. **Continuity of Purpose** – ensuring that the company's mission, values, and long-term objectives remain intact despite leadership changes.
2. **Stability of Operations** – minimizing disruptions to customers, employees, and stakeholders.
3. **Credibility and Trust** – maintaining the confidence of investors, regulators, and markets during uncertain times.
4. **Strategic Renewal** – using the transition period as an

opportunity to introduce fresh perspectives, new competencies, and innovation.

Corporate governance frameworks see transitional leadership as more than succession planning. It is not only about "who will sit in the chair," but about "how the organisation moves from one chair to the next without falling apart."

Boards of directors, investors, and regulators value transitional leadership because it reduces the risks associated with dependency on a single individual. A well-designed transition strategy reassures stakeholders that the organisation is bigger than any one leader.

Difference Between Temporary Management, Succession, and Transformational Leadership

When organisations reach a point of leadership change, whether through the founder stepping down, a CEO resigning, or a generational shift in ownership, they enter one of the most vulnerable phases of their existence. The direction taken in this period often determines whether the company flourishes into an enduring institution or collapses into memory. This is where **transitional leadership** becomes critical.

Transitional leadership is not just about finding a replacement for the leader. It is about creating the bridge between the old and the new, ensuring continuity while enabling necessary change. It requires a careful balance: preserving the company's essence while adapting it for the future.

What Transitional Leadership Means in Corporate Governance

In the context of corporate governance, transitional leadership is the structured approach to managing leadership change within an organisation. It emphasizes:

- **Continuity of Purpose**: Ensuring that the company's mission, values, and long-term objectives remain intact despite leadership changes.
- **Stability of Operations**: Minimizing disruptions to customers, employees, and stakeholders.
- **Credibility and Trust**: Maintaining the confidence of investors, regulators, and markets during uncertain times.
- **Strategic Renewal**: Using the transition period as an opportunity to introduce fresh perspectives, new competencies, and innovation.

Corporate governance frameworks see transitional leadership as more than succession planning. It is not only about "who will sit in the chair," but about "how the organisation moves from one chair to the next without falling apart." Boards of directors, investors, and regulators value transitional leadership because it reduces the risks associated with dependency on a single individual. A well-designed transition strategy reassures stakeholders that the organisation is bigger than any one leader.

The Difference Between Temporary Management, Succession, Transformational, and Transitional Leadership

It's easy to confuse transitional leadership with related concepts, but they are distinct, and understanding the differences is vital.

1. <u>Temporary Management</u>: Temporary management is reactive. It happens when a leader suddenly exits, due to resignation, illness, or death, and someone is appointed to "hold the fort." The goal is stability, not transformation.

- **Example**: After the sudden resignation of former CEO Mark Fields in 2017, the Ford Motor Company board appointed Jim Hackett as a temporary CEO to stabilize operations and provide a clear direction before a permanent successor was chosen. His role was to "hold the fort" while the board planned for a long-term solution.

2. **Succession:** Succession is a planned process of identifying and grooming a new leader well in advance, ensuring they are ready when the current leader steps aside. It emphasizes preparedness and continuity, often within family businesses or long-standing corporations.

   - **Example**: When Howard Schultz returned to Starbucks as CEO in 2022, he did so with the explicit goal of preparing for a seamless transition. He worked to train his hand-picked successor, Laxman Narasimhan, ensuring Narasimhan was ready to take the reins and continue the company's long-term vision. This planned approach ensured the company's stability during a crucial period.

3. **Transformational Leadership:** Transformational leadership is visionary. It is about inspiring teams, driving change, and achieving extraordinary performance. This leadership style emphasizes long-term innovation, cultural transformation, and motivating individuals to exceed expectations.

   - **Example**: Satya Nadella's leadership at Microsoft is a prime example. He successfully transformed Microsoft's culture from a competitive internal environment to one focused on collaboration and innovation. He also shifted the company's strategy from a Windows-first approach to a cloud-first vision, demonstrating how a visionary leader can redefine an organisation's core business and values.

4. **Transitional Leadership:** Transitional leadership is strategic. It is the bridge that connects the other three concepts. It maintains immediate stability through temporary management, prepares the next generation of leaders through succession planning, and fosters renewal and innovation

through transformational leadership. Its dual focus is what makes it unique: protecting the past while securing the future.

- o **Example**: The transition from Indra Nooyi to Ramon Laguarta at PepsiCo is a good illustration. Nooyi stepped down after a successful tenure, but she didn't just hand over the reins. The company executed a well-planned transition that allowed Laguarta to shadow her, gain an understanding of the company's complex global operations, and prepare for the role. This transitional period ensured a smooth handover of power, allowing the new leader to begin implementing their own strategic vision without disrupting the company's momentum.

Transitional Leadership as a Bridge Between Founder-Driven and Institution-Driven Organisations

Most founder-led companies are deeply personal. They reflect the founder's values, personality, and energy. Decisions are centralised, often informal, and sometimes emotional. This model is effective in the early stages, but as the company expands, it becomes unsustainable.

Institution-driven organisations, on the other hand, operate on systems, governance, and culture. Leadership becomes transferable. The organisation has codified policies, documented strategies, and independent boards that ensure continuity.

Transitional leadership is the bridge between these two realities.

It allows companies to:

1. **Move from personality to process** – ensuring decisions are not dependent on one individual.
   Example: The transition at Google from the founders'

11

hands-on, intuitive decisions to Sundar Pichai's more structured, process-driven leadership. The founders, Larry Page and Sergey Brin, were known for their informal leadership. As CEO, Pichai formalized decision-making, relying on a structured, cross-functional review process and more formalized project management, ensuring the company could scale without being tied to a small group of leaders.

2. **Shift from vision to governance** – turning founder dreams into structured, board-monitored strategies.

   Example: After Tesla became a publicly traded company, Elon Musk's visionary goals had to be balanced with corporate governance. The board of directors, institutional investors, and public reporting requirements play a crucial role in guiding and monitoring the company's strategic direction. This shift ensures the company's long-term sustainability by translating the founder's vision into a formalized, accountable strategy.

3. **Evolve from dependency to resilience** – building leadership pipelines and systems that can withstand leadership changes.
   Example: Apple's planned transition from Steve Jobs to Tim Cook is a perfect illustration. While Jobs was the charismatic visionary, the company's resilience was built on its deep leadership pipeline and established operational excellence. This intentional approach allowed Apple to not only survive the loss of its founder but to flourish, becoming one of the world's most valuable companies.

Without transitional leadership, most companies get stuck in the founder-driven stage. With it, companies cross into becoming enduring institutions that can see second, third, and even fourth generations of leadership.

The Heart of Transitional Leadership

At its core, transitional leadership is about one thing: business continuity. It is the intentional practice of ensuring the business survives beyond its founder, its first CEO, or any charismatic leader. It is the art of leadership that hands over the baton without breaking the race.

And for founders, it requires humility, the willingness to accept that the most significant measure of their success is not how well they run the business today, but how well it runs when they are no longer there.

Chapter 3
THE COST OF FOUNDER DEPENDENCY

Behind every thriving startup is usually a determined founder who fought through storms to bring the company to life. Their story is often heroic: they mortgaged their homes, worked sleepless nights, and made sacrifices that others would never dare. Their grit is what gave birth to the company. But as much as this story inspires, it often becomes the same reason the company struggles to survive without them. Founder dependency, when an organisation is overly reliant on the personality, decisions, and presence of its founder, is a hidden time bomb that eventually explodes.

Why Founder-Centric Leadership Creates Hidden Risks

At first, founder dependency feels harmless. Employees take pride in working closely with a visionary leader. Customers are drawn to the founder's charisma. Investors appreciate their relentless drive. The founder becomes the face, voice, and soul of the company.

But as the company grows, this dependency turns into a liability:

- Decision Bottlenecks: Every decision, big or small, must pass through the founder. This slows execution, frustrates teams, and creates a culture of waiting rather than thinking.
- Lack of Institutional Knowledge: Strategies, customer relationships, and operational know-how live in the founder's head. Without proper documentation and delegation, the company has no "memory" outside of the founder.

- Fragile Employee Morale: Employees feel insecure because their jobs seem tied to the founder's presence. The moment the founder is absent, morale drops and turnover spikes.
- Investor Hesitancy: Smart investors know the danger of founder dependency. They hesitate to fund companies that cannot operate independently, no matter how innovative the product may be.
- Operational Collapse: If the founder falls ill, retires, or suddenly passes away, the entire business risks collapsing because no system exists for continuity.

In essence, the founder becomes both the most significant asset and the biggest risk.

The Real Cost of Founder Dependency

When all is said and done, founder dependency costs companies not just financially but existentially. It destroys continuity. It leaves employees jobless, investors betrayed, customers abandoned, and entire industries weaker.

Example: A prominent tech startup, known for its charismatic founder's relentless drive, raised millions and experienced exponential growth. But the founder was the sole decision-maker, and all key relationships were centralised with them. When a sudden health crisis forced the founder into a prolonged absence, the company ground to a halt. Projects stalled, teams became directionless, and key partnerships unraveled. Within months, the company was forced to shut down, leaving employees without jobs and investors with a total loss. The brilliant idea was viable, but the business itself was not resilient.

The bitter truth is that if a company cannot live without its founder, it was never truly built to last. This is why transitional leadership is not optional; it is essential. It is the only way to transform businesses from fragile founder-centric entities into enduring institutions.

Stories of Companies That Collapsed After Founder Exit

The world of business offers countless cautionary tales.

1. Polaroid: Founded by Edwin Land, Polaroid was a giant in instant photography. Land was the visionary and the innovator. But after his departure, Polaroid lost its way. Without Land's singular leadership and with no strong governance structures to ensure innovation continued, the company collapsed, eventually filing for bankruptcy in 2001.
2. Chickadee Family Businesses (Generic Example): Across emerging markets, thousands of family-owned businesses vanish after their founders die. These were businesses that employed hundreds and supported entire communities. However, with no leadership pipeline, board structures, or transition plan, they dissolved within months of the founder's passing.
3. Pan Am Airways: At one time, Pan Am was the most famous airline in the world, driven by the forceful leadership of Juan Trippe. But when Trippe stepped down, the airline, heavily dependent on his vision and connections, struggled to adapt. By 1991, Pan Am collapsed, despite its legacy as a global pioneer.

These stories are not just about failure. They are warnings. They remind us that no company can thrive indefinitely if its lifeblood is concentrated in one person.

Psychological and Emotional Barriers Founders Face in Letting Go

If founder dependency is so dangerous, why do so many companies fall into it? The answer lies in the psychology of founders.

- Identity Fusion: For many founders, the company is not just a business; it is an extension of themselves. They cannot imagine separating their personal identity from the organisation they built.
- Fear of Irrelevance: Stepping back feels like disappearing. Founders often fear that once they leave, their relevance will fade, and their life's work will be forgotten.
- Distrust of Others: Founders frequently struggle to believe anyone else can run the business as well as they can. Even when competent leaders are available, they hesitate to hand over authority.
- Perfectionism and Control: Years of doing everything themselves build a habit of micromanagement. The idea of delegating feels risky, and they worry that letting go means compromising quality control.
- Emotional Attachment: Businesses often carry sentimental value. They remind the founder of sacrifices, failures, and triumphs. This emotional weight makes it incredibly hard to imagine someone else taking over.

These psychological barriers are real and deeply human. Yet, if they are not addressed, they become the silent assassins of continuity.

Chapter 4
LAYING THE FOUNDATION FOR AN ORGANISATION THAT OUTLIVES YOU

A company's survival is not guaranteed by how profitable it is today, but by how well it has been structured to endure tomorrow. Too many founders build successful businesses only to watch them collapse because the foundation was designed for a person, not an institution. If you want your company to outlive you, you must lay the groundwork from the beginning, not when you are about to retire, but from the very first day you put an idea on paper. This chapter examines the fundamental building blocks of creating an organisation that thrives long after the founder has passed away.

Vision vs. Systems: Institutionalizing Culture and Mission

Most founders start with a clear vision, a mental picture of the impact they want to create. The vision fuels energy, attracts talent, and inspires early customers. But vision alone is not enough. Without systems, vision dies with the visionary.

Codify the Vision

- Write it down. Build mission and vision statements that every employee can repeat and align with.
- Translate values into policies and daily practices, not just posters on the wall.

Example: Patagonia, the outdoor apparel company, famously codified its vision to "Build the best product, cause no unnecessary harm, use business to inspire and implement solutions to the environmental crisis." This isn't just a slogan; it's a living document that guides every business decision, from material sourcing to supply chain practices.

Build Systems That Carry the Vision

- Create organisational processes (for decision-making, hiring, customer service) that reflect your values.
- Develop onboarding **programme**s that indoctrinate new employees into the company's culture.
- Document workflows so that the company's DNA is not trapped in the founder's brain.

Example: At Amazon, Jeff Bezos's core value of "customer obsession" was institutionalized through processes like the "two-pizza team" rule (teams must be small enough to be fed by two pizzas to ensure agility) and the practice of writing a six-page "press release" for any new product or initiative. This forces teams to work backward from the customer's perspective, ensuring that the company's DNA of customer focus endures, regardless of who is in charge.

Culture as an Operating System

- Think of culture not as "vibes" but as the software that runs the company.
- Culture should dictate how people behave when no one is watching, ensuring alignment even after leadership changes.

Example: The Netflix Culture Deck is a prime example of a company making its culture an operating system. The document explicitly defines their values (such as "courage," "selflessness," and "candor") and the behaviours expected of employees. This system enables Netflix to maintain its unique, high-performance culture as it expands to thousands of employees worldwide, ensuring that the company's institutional memory is preserved.

When vision is aligned with systems, culture becomes institutionalized. It stops being yours and starts being the company's.

Structuring for Scale: From "One-Man Business" to Enduring Company

Many businesses die because they remain one-man empires disguised as companies. If every client depends on you, if every decision ends at your desk, and if every crisis waits for your approval, then you don't have a company, you have a job with employees.

To transition into an enduring company, the structure must evolve:

Delegate Decision-Making

- Empower managers to make independent decisions.
- Establish clear reporting lines and accountability structures.

Example: A founder might create a "leadership scorecard" that gives each department head a clear set of metrics for success (e.g., customer satisfaction, product uptime, sales targets). By empowering them with ownership and tying their success to these metrics, the founder can step back and focus on high-level strategy, trusting that the teams are making the right day-to-day decisions.

Build a Real Leadership Team

- Invest in hiring strong executives (for finance, operations, marketing) who can run the business without your micromanagement.
- Encourage healthy conflict and diverse perspectives at the top.

Example: Steve Jobs, a visionary focused on product design and user experience, brought in Tim Cook, a master of supply chain and operations. Their complementary skills created an executive team that was far more powerful than either could have been alone. By building a team with diverse strengths, Jobs ensured that the company had the institutional capacity to execute on his vision.

Formalize Governance

- Move from founder control to shared control with a board of directors or advisors.
- Independent voices bring stability and credibility.

Example: As a tech company grows, a founder might transition from a small, informal advisory group to a formal board of directors. This board, which includes outside experts and investors, provides strategic oversight, holds the leadership team accountable, and ensures the company is making decisions that benefit all stakeholders, not just the founder.

Separate Founder from Company Brand

- Let the company's name and identity shine brighter than your personal identity.
- Customers should trust the company, not just the founder.

Example: When Jeff Bezos stepped down as CEO of Amazon, the company's brand and operational identity were so strong that the transition was seamless. Customers continued to rely on Amazon's services, and investors maintained confidence in its direction because the company's core principles—customer obsession, long-term thinking, and a focus on operational excellence—were deeply ingrained in its culture and systems, not just tied to Bezos himself.

Scaling is not just about adding employees or revenue. It is about designing the company to exist without you.

Early-Stage Decisions That Affect Long-Term Sustainability

Founders often underestimate the importance of early

decisions in determining whether their company can transition into an institution. Small choices, made in the frantic pace of a startup, compound over time and ultimately create the foundation for either a resilient company or a fragile one. The following are critical areas where foresight in the early days can make all the difference in the company's long-term sustainability.

Ownership and Equity Structure

- Bringing in co-founders, early investors, or offering employee stock options creates a shared responsibility and fosters long-term buy-in.
- Avoid keeping 100% control at all costs; it may feel secure, but it breeds fragility and makes it impossible to build a broad base of support.

Example: The founders of Google, Larry Page and Sergey Brin, brought in venture capitalists and other key executives early on. This distributed ownership and responsibility ensured that when the company went public, a broad base of stakeholders was invested in its long-term success.

Financial Transparency

- Adopt strong accounting practices from day one.
- Build trust with stakeholders through transparent reporting.
- Without this, transitions become messy and unattractive to successors or investors, as they have no clear view of the company's health.

Example: Early-stage companies that use professional accounting software and a transparent budget management process build a foundation of trust. When it's time to raise a new round of funding or hand over the reins, these clean financial records make the company a far more attractive and credible prospect to investors and potential successors.

Talent Development

- From the start, invest in training and developing your team, rather than simply hiring for immediate needs.
- A pipeline of leaders inside the company reduces the shock of leadership changes and ensures institutional knowledge is preserved.

Example: Companies like General Electric, under the leadership of Jack Welch, were renowned for their internal leadership development **programme**s. Welch's "A-players, B-players, C-players" framework for evaluating talent, while controversial, institutionalized a culture of constant performance review and talent cultivation. This created a deep bench of qualified leaders ready to take on new roles, ensuring the company's stability.

Documentation and Knowledge Management

- Early-stage founders often run on memory. But without documentation, the company loses direction when the founder exits.
- Start building manuals, policies, and records that can outlive people. This is how a company's "DNA" is institutionalized.

Example: The co-founders of Airbnb, Joe Gebbia and Brian Chesky, famously documented the company's early culture in a document called the "Airbnb Culture Book." This document, which outlined their core values and beliefs, served as a foundational text that could be shared with new employees and leaders, ensuring that the company's ethos remained intact as it grew into a global enterprise.

Customer Relationships Beyond the Founder

- Don't make the mistake of being the only person clients trust.
- Create customer service systems, account managers, and communication channels that allow customers to trust the organisation, not just you. This builds a brand that can survive and thrive after you leave.

Example: Zappos built its entire brand around the concept of legendary customer service. While founder Tony Hsieh was a well-known figure, the company's success was not tied to his personal relationships with customers. Instead, it was built on a system of empowered customer service representatives who were trusted to go above and beyond, ensuring that customer loyalty was directed toward the company itself.

The Founder's Dilemma

Founders must make peace with a hard truth: if everything depends on you, you are not building a company, you are bottlenecking it.

Building for continuity requires humility. It means accepting that your most significant achievement is not being indispensable, but making yourself unnecessary. It means celebrating when your company functions better without your daily involvement.

This shift is what turns fragile businesses into enduring institutions. It is what allows companies to see second, third, and even fourth generations of leadership without losing their soul.

The Foundation of Legacy

Ultimately, laying the foundation for an enduring organisation is about choosing legacy over control. It is about building structures that ensure your vision outlives your name and your impact continues long after you are gone.

The companies that endure are not those with the strongest founders, but those with the strongest foundations.

Chapter 5
CORPORATE GOVERNANCE AS THE BACKBONE OF TRANSITION

No company can transition from being founder-led to institution-led without a solid governance framework. Governance is the backbone that holds the company steady during moments of uncertainty, ensuring that leadership changes do not derail its mission, culture, or operations.

Corporate governance, simply put, is the system of rules, processes, and relationships by which a company is directed and controlled. While founders often view governance as a burden or a distraction from innovation, the truth is that good governance is the difference between companies that collapse when a leader exits and those that thrive for generations.

The Role of Boards, Advisors, and Governance Frameworks

1. Board of Directors

The board is not meant to rubber-stamp the founder's decisions. It exists to:

- Provide strategic direction beyond the founder's personal vision.
- Hold leadership accountable to shareholders, employees, and stakeholders.
- Safeguard continuity by ensuring succession plans are in place.

In companies that endure, the board acts as the guardian of continuity. It bridges the gap between founders and future leadership, ensuring that transitions are guided by systems, not emotions.

Example: When Disney's founder, Walt Disney, passed away, the company's board of directors, including his brother Roy O. Disney, was crucial in steering the company through the transition. By upholding the company's established vision and ensuring continuity in its creative and business leadership, they preserved the company's legacy and allowed it to flourish for decades.

2. Advisors and Mentors

Advisory boards and mentors complement formal boards by:

- Offering **specialised** expertise (technology, finance, markets).
- Acting as sounding boards for leadership decisions.
- Guiding founders to think institutionally, not personally.

Advisors often help founders evolve from being operators to institution-builders, reminding them that their legacy depends on shared leadership.

Example: As a startup founder scales their company, they might bring on an advisory board with experts in specific fields like enterprise sales or international expansion. These advisors provide **specialised**, real-world advice that a generalist board might not possess, helping the founder navigate complex challenges and avoid common pitfalls, ultimately building a more robust and sustainable business.

3. Governance Frameworks

Governance is not just about having a board; it is about frameworks that define how decisions are made, who is accountable, and how performance is measured. These frameworks are what turn fragile businesses into enduring institutions.

Strong frameworks include:

- **Bylaws and constitutions** that define roles, powers, and responsibilities.
- **Succession policies** that prepare for planned and unplanned exits.
- **Risk management systems** that anticipate crises before they occur.
- **Ethics codes and compliance structures** that uphold trust across generations.

Example: A family-owned business might create a formal succession policy that outlines the criteria for a future CEO and establishes a clear timeline for the transition. This framework prevents potential family conflicts and ensures the business's long-term health by prioritizing a merit-based approach, guaranteeing a smooth and professional handoff.

The Importance of Independent Directors

One of the most powerful features of governance is independence. Independent directors—board members who are neither employees, founders, nor major shareholders—bring objectivity to leadership transitions.

Why They Matter:

1. Unbiased Oversight

- Independent directors evaluate leadership without personal or financial bias.
- They ensure that decisions are made in the company's best interest, not just the founder's.

Example: During a critical negotiation for a company acquisition, an independent director can provide an unbiased perspective on the deal's fairness, ensuring the founder's emotional attachment to the company doesn't lead to a poor financial decision.

2. Credibility with Investors

- Investors and regulators are reassured when governance includes independent voices.
- Independence signals that the company is bigger than one personality, which is a key indicator of stability.

Example: When a startup is seeking a new round of funding, the presence of a well-respected independent director on the board gives investors confidence that the company's financial and strategic health is being managed professionally and not just by the whim of the founder.

3. Succession Neutrality

- During transitions, independent directors prevent **favouritism** or emotional decision-making.
- They help ensure the best successor is chosen based on competence, not loyalty.

Example: When a founder is retiring, a board with a strong independent director can lead the search for a new CEO. This ensures the selection process is based on objective criteria, such as past performance and strategic vision, rather than on who the founder feels most comfortable with.

4. Crisis Management

- In turbulent times, independent directors provide calm, experienced guidance.
- Their external perspective is often what stabilizes organisations in transition.

Example: If a company faces a public scandal, an independent director can step in to lead the crisis response, providing a credible, neutral voice to the media and the public, which helps to protect the company's reputation.

A board without independent directors risks becoming an echo chamber for the founder's voice. A board with them becomes an institution capable of outliving its founders.

Checks and Balances Beyond the Founder's Authority

Founders often struggle with the idea of being checked. After all, they built the company, sacrificed for it, and carried it to success. But unchecked founder power creates fragility. Checks and balances are not about undermining the founders; they are about protecting the company.

Distributed Authority

- Decision-making should not be centralised in the founder's office.
- Executive committees, boards, and managers should share responsibility.

Example: Instead of the founder approving every new product feature, the company can establish a product committee that includes engineers, marketers, and designers. This ensures those make decisions with the most relevant expertise and prevents the founder from becoming a bottleneck.

Transparency and Accountability

- Regular audits, performance reviews, and financial reporting ensure leadership is answerable.
- Accountability builds trust and reduces risk during transitions.

Example: Companies that have a clear system for reporting financial performance to the board every quarter are more likely to catch issues early. This transparency builds trust with all stakeholders and makes any leadership transition more seamless, as the company's health is clear to everyone.

Employee Voice

- Governance should allow employee feedback to influence leadership, preventing cultures of silence.
- Engaged employees are more likely to stay during transitions, providing invaluable institutional knowledge.

Example: Implementing an anonymous feedback system or creating an employee-led advisory council can give employees a direct line to leadership. This helps the company identify and address issues that the founder might not be aware of, preventing turnover and maintaining morale during periods of change.

Legal and Regulatory Compliance

- Governance ensures the company respects the laws of its jurisdiction.
- Without compliance, transitions become legal and reputational nightmares.

Example: A company might implement a formal compliance training **programme** for all employees and executives. This ensures that everyone understands their legal obligations, from data privacy to labor laws, which protects the company from costly lawsuits and reputational damage as it grows and changes.

In short, checks and balances make sure that no one person, not even the founder, is bigger than the company.

Governance as the Foundation of Legacy

At its core, governance is about designing a company that can be trusted to endure, with or without its founder. It is about creating structures where leadership transitions are not moments of chaos but natural phases of growth.

Every company that has lasted more than a century, IBM, Procter & Gamble, Unilever, Nestlé, shares one thing in common: strong governance. Their founders are long gone, but their governance frameworks ensure new leaders emerge, new strategies evolve, and the mission continues.

For founders who want to build legacies, governance is not optional. It is the backbone that ensures the company does not die with them.

Chapter 6
THE ROLE OF INVESTORS, PARTNERS, AND CO-FOUNDERS

No company that outlives its founder is built in isolation. While founders often carry the initial vision, it is the involvement of external stakeholders, investors, partners, and co-founders that transforms a fragile idea into a resilient institution. These stakeholders provide what founders alone cannot: capital, expertise, accountability, and continuity.

Why Involving External Stakeholders Matters

The temptation for many founders is to "go it alone." They fear losing control, diluting ownership, or sharing credit. But clinging to total control often becomes the very reason the company cannot survive their absence.

External stakeholders matter because they:

1. **Reduce Founder Dependency**
    o   Investors, partners, and co-founders create a shared leadership model.
    o   They ensure the company's direction does not depend on a single individual.

Example: The co-founders of Airbnb, Brian Chesky, Joe Gebbia, and Nathan Blecharczyk, each brought a unique skill set to the company, from design and product vision to technical expertise. Their shared leadership ensured that the company was not reliant on a single person for all key decisions, making it more resilient and adaptable as it grew.

2. Strengthen Decision-Making

- o With diverse perspectives, decisions are no longer based solely on the founder's instincts.
- o External voices challenge assumptions and provide balance.

Example: When launching a new product, a founder's instincts might favor speed over perfection. An external investor with a background in regulatory compliance might insist on a more cautious approach, helping the company avoid future legal issues and ensuring the product is built on a solid, long-term foundation.

3. Ensure Continuity During Transitions

- o If the founder exits, the stakeholders remain, providing stability until new leadership is established.

Example: After the founders of PayPal, including Elon Musk, Peter Thiel, and Max Levchin, moved on, the company's investors and board of directors provided the necessary stability. Their collective experience and governance ensured that the company's operations and strategy remained on track, allowing it to eventually be acquired by eBay for a massive sum.

4. Build Market Confidence

- o Customers, employees, and investors trust organisations with strong, visible stakeholders.
- o It signals that the company is an institution, not a personality cult.

Example: When Satya Nadella took over as CEO of Microsoft from Steve Ballmer, the company's strong board and institutional investor base provided confidence to the market. This signaled that the company's future was not dependent on a single personality, but rather on a well-structured and transparent governance system.

Put simply, external stakeholders are the insurance policy for a company's longevity.

Capital, Expertise, and Accountability

1. **Capital** Growth requires resources. Investors bring financial backing that ensures the company can scale, expand, and survive shocks. More importantly, capital from external investors binds the company to structures of accountability, reducing the risk of reckless decision-making.

Expertise: No founder knows everything. Co-founders and partners bring complementary strengths, technical knowledge, operational skills, or market access that the founder alone cannot provide.

- A visionary may need a strong operator.
- A product genius may need a financial strategist.
- A risk-taker may need a cautious partner.

This combination creates balance, making the company less vulnerable to one person's blind spots.

2. **Accountability** External stakeholders demand discipline. They ask hard questions. They review numbers. They hold leaders responsible. While this may frustrate founders, it forces companies to adopt governance structures that outlive individual personalities. Without accountability, companies drift into founder dependency. With it, they evolve into institutions.

Case Studies of Companies Where Investor Involvement Ensured Continuity

1. Apple

When Steve Jobs left Apple in 1985, the company struggled. But after his return in 1997, he transformed Apple into one of the greatest companies of all time. When Jobs passed away in 2011, many feared Apple would collapse without him. But the company's institutional investors and structured board insisted on continuity. With Tim Cook's steady leadership, Apple not only survived but became the world's most valuable company. Jobs built the vision; investors and governance structures ensured the vision outlived him.

2. Google (Alphabet)

Larry Page and Sergey Brin, the co-founders of Google, made an intentional decision early on: they would not run Google forever. By bringing in Eric Schmidt as CEO in 2001 and later restructuring into Alphabet with a strong board and investor presence, they ensured Google's growth beyond themselves. Today, Sundar Pichai leads Alphabet, proving that Google is no longer just "Larry and Sergey's company," but a global institution.

3. Disney

Walt Disney was a creative genius, but his brother Roy Disney and early investors provided the financial and operational grounding that turned the dream into an empire. Even after Walt died in 1966, the involvement of external leaders and investors allowed Disney to continue expanding, acquiring Pixar, Marvel, and Lucasfilm decades later. Disney outlived its founder because it was never built on one man alone.

4. Dangote Group (Africa)

Aliko Dangote built Africa's largest conglomerate, but what made the company sustainable was not just his vision. It was the involvement of investors, partners, and professional executives who managed various subsidiaries with accountability. By spreading decision-making and involving external oversight, Dangote Group became an institution, not just a founder's empire.

The Founder's Dilemma with Stakeholders

Many founders resist involving external stakeholders for fear of:

- Losing control.
- Diluting equity.
- Being questioned or challenged.

But what they fail to realize is this: the price of 100% control is often 0% continuity. By sharing ownership and authority, founders trade a slice of control for the survival of their vision. The question is not whether you want control today, but whether you want a company that still exists tomorrow.

The Power of Shared Leadership

The companies that survive generations are not those with the strongest founders, but those with shared leadership structures.

- **Investors** bring the discipline of accountability.
- **Partners** bring complementary expertise.
- **Co-founders** bring balance and succession readiness.

Together, they transform a business from fragile to enduring.

Building Beyond Yourself

As a founder, your greatest achievement is not building a company you alone can lead. It is building one that continues to thrive when you are gone. That cannot happen without external stakeholders. Legacy is not preserved by control; it is preserved by collaboration. The sooner founders embrace investors, partners, and co-founders, the sooner they begin building institutions that truly outlive them.

Chapter 7
SUCCESSION PLANNING AND LEADERSHIP PIPELINES

If there is one word that separates fragile businesses from enduring institutions, it is **succession**. Succession planning is the art of ensuring that the departure of a leader, whether planned or unplanned, does not disrupt the survival of the organisation.

Many companies avoid the conversation because it feels uncomfortable, even disloyal, to imagine a founder or CEO no longer in place. Yet the companies that thrive across generations are those that treat succession not as a taboo but as a core strategic function.

Identifying and Grooming Successors Internally

The most effective successions often come from within. Organisations that survive transitions are deliberate in identifying high-potential leaders early and creating clear pathways for them to grow.

1. **Spotting Potential Early**

   o Look beyond current performance. Future leaders often reveal themselves not only in results but in curiosity, resilience, and the ability to influence others.

   o Use talent reviews, 360-degree feedback, and leadership assessments to identify individuals with long-term potential.

   o **Example**: A project manager who consistently asks insightful questions about the company's long-term strategy, even when it's outside their direct role, may

37

have the makings of a future leader. Identifying this curiosity and giving them opportunities to engage in strategic discussions is a key part of spotting potential early.

2. Progressive Responsibility

- Gradually expose potential successors to increasing levels of responsibility.

- Rotate them across functions—finance, operations, strategy—so they develop a broad view of the organisation.

- **Example**: A high-potential marketing manager might be given a 6-month assignment in the finance department to learn about budgeting and resource allocation. This experience not only broadens their skill set but also gives them a better understanding of how the different parts of the business work together.

3. Shadowing and Exposure

- Allow successors to shadow senior leaders in key meetings and decisions.

- Involve them in board interactions, investor discussions, and major strategic reviews to prepare them for the realities of leadership.

- **Example**: A CEO might invite a potential successor to sit in on board meetings as an observer. This provides them with an understanding of how the board operates and the kinds of questions it asks, preparing them for the intense scrutiny that comes with a top leadership role.

The goal is simple: by the time a successor takes the helm, they should already be familiar with the weight of leadership.

Building Leadership Development Programmes

Leadership does not happen by accident. It must be designed. Building structured **programme**s within the organisation ensures a continuous pipeline of capable leaders ready for transition.

1. Formal Training Programmes

- o Internal academies or partnerships with business schools to sharpen managerial and leadership skills.

- o **Programme**s on finance, governance, strategy, and digital transformation.

- o **Example**: Many large corporations, like GE and Johnson & Johnson, run internal leadership academies. These **programme**s use a blend of classroom learning, case studies, and mentorship to systematically train a new generation of leaders.

2. Stretch Assignments

- o Assign high-potential leaders to challenging projects that test resilience, problem-solving, and innovation.

- o Examples: launching a new market, managing a turnaround, or leading a cross-border initiative.

- o **Example**: A rising star in the product team might be given the difficult task of launching a new product in a challenging market, forcing them to learn how to navigate cultural differences, logistical hurdles, and competitive pressures.

3. Succession Bench Strength

- o Don't rely on one "chosen heir." Build a bench of leaders so that the organisation has multiple options.

- o This reduces dependency on one individual and ensures continuity if a successor exits unexpectedly.

- o **Example**: A company might have a list of three potential candidates for every senior leadership role, each with a detailed development plan. This "bench" ensures that if the primary candidate leaves, there are other qualified individuals ready to step up, preventing a leadership vacuum.

4. Performance + Values Alignment

- o True successors are not only skilled but also embody the company's values and culture.

- o Leadership pipelines should screen for both technical competence and cultural fit.

- o **Example**: When assessing a candidate for a leadership role, a company might use a 360-degree feedback process to evaluate not only their results but also how they achieved them, ensuring their actions align with the company's core values, like teamwork or integrity.

An organisation that trains leaders at every level is one that never runs out of leadership.

The Role of Mentorship, Executive Coaching, and Deliberate Succession

1. Strategy **Mentorship**

   - Senior leaders must actively mentor future successors, passing down wisdom, networks, and institutional knowledge.

   - Mentorship reduces the "experience gap" that successors often face.

   - **Example**: A senior executive might take a high-potential manager under their wing, meeting with them monthly to discuss challenges, offer advice, and introduce them to key contacts. This informal relationship provides invaluable guidance that formal training cannot replicate.

2. **Executive Coaching**

   - Professional coaching accelerates the development of leadership capacity.

   - Coaches help successors refine emotional intelligence, resilience, and decision-making.

   - **Example**: A new manager might work with an executive coach to improve their communication skills, especially in high-pressure situations. The coach can provide objective feedback and actionable strategies to help the manager grow into their new role.

3. **Deliberate Succession Strategy**

   - Succession must be formalized, not left to chance. A written strategy should define:

o   Who the potential successors are.

o   What development plans are in place.

o   What the process will be in the event of planned or emergency exits.

o   **Example**: A board might have a sealed, confidential document that outlines a clear succession plan, including who will take over on an interim basis and a list of internal and external candidates, to be used in the event of the CEO's sudden departure.

4. **Communication and Transparency**

o   Employees and stakeholders need to trust that leadership transitions are not chaotic.

o   A transparent process reassures markets, investors, and teams that the company is stable.

o   **Example**: When a long-time CEO announces their retirement, the company can publicly communicate the succession plan, outlining the timeline and the process for selecting a new leader. This transparency reduces uncertainty and prevents speculation, which helps maintain employee morale and market confidence.

Case Example: General Electric (GE)

For decades, GE was seen as a masterclass in succession planning. Leaders like Jack Welch spent years grooming successors through rotations, mentorship, and leadership development **programme**s. He famously had a "C-suite" plan where he would actively assess and rank potential successors, ensuring a deep bench of talent. While not without challenges, GE's structured approach ensured that leadership transitions were rarely surprises, and successors were battle-tested long before assuming the role. This methodical approach to leadership development allowed GE to maintain its position as a global industrial leader for decades.

The Cost of Neglecting Succession

Organisations that ignore succession often face chaos when leadership changes:

- Internal power struggles.

- Talent exodus due to uncertainty.

- Loss of investor and customer confidence.

- Risk of collapse during unexpected founder exits.

Succession planning is not an act of pessimism; it is an act of **stewardship**. It signals that the founder or CEO values the company's future more than their own position.

Leadership Beyond a Lifetime

Succession is not about replacing a leader. It is about ensuring the organisation remains resilient, credible, and forward-looking regardless of who sits in the corner office.

By identifying and grooming successors, building leadership pipelines, and embedding mentorship and coaching, companies prepare for the future with confidence. The ultimate test of leadership is not how well you lead today, but how well the company leads when you are gone.

Chapter 8
THE INTERIM CEO AND TRANSITIONAL EXECUTIVES

Leadership transitions are rarely seamless. Sometimes they are carefully planned, but many times, they are sudden, forced, or turbulent. A founder resigns unexpectedly, a CEO is removed by the board, or a crisis demands a leadership shift no one anticipated. In such moments, organisations face a dangerous vacuum at the top—a vacuum that, if left unfilled, can destroy trust, paralyze operations, and send shockwaves through employees and stakeholders.

This is where interim CEOs and transitional executives step in. Their role is not to permanently redefine the company but to stabilize, steward, and prepare the ground for long-term leadership. They are temporary stewards who act as a bridge, ensuring continuity while the organisation recalibrates.

When and Why Transitional Leaders Are Necessary

Transitional leaders are not a one-size-fits-all solution, but they become invaluable in several key situations.

1. Sudden Leadership Vacancies

When a CEO resigns, passes away, or is removed unexpectedly, a leadership vacuum can create panic. An interim leader prevents this by ensuring day-to-day operations continue without disruption.

- **Example:** When the CEO of a major tech company suddenly resigned due to a personal scandal, the board immediately appointed a former COO as interim CEO. This move sent a clear message to the market and employees: the company had

44

a steady hand at the helm, and its strategy would not be derailed.

2. Restructuring and Turnarounds

Companies undergoing mergers, acquisitions, or financial crises often need a leader who specializes in stabilizing organisations in flux. A transitional executive can make tough, impartial decisions necessary for a turnaround.

- **Example:** A legacy retail chain was on the brink of bankruptcy. The board brought in a seasoned turnaround specialist as an interim CEO. This executive quickly negotiated with creditors, closed unprofitable stores, and streamlined the supply chain, creating a healthier foundation for a permanent leader to build upon.

3. Cultural Realignment

When an organisation has been overly dependent on a founder or a long-serving CEO, the culture can become stagnant. A transitional leader helps reset the company culture, preparing it for a new era.

- **Example:** Following the departure of a beloved but autocratic founder, an interim CEO was appointed to decentralize decision-making. They introduced a new system of project teams and empowered middle managers, shifting the culture from a top-down hierarchy to a more collaborative and innovative environment.

4. Buying Time for Succession

Boards may need time to identify, vet, and groom the right long-term leader. An interim CEO provides the necessary breathing space to make thoughtful, deliberate decisions rather than a rushed and potentially poor choice.

- **Example:** A major pharmaceutical company's CEO

announced his retirement, but his heir apparent was still a year away from being ready to take the reins. An interim leader was appointed to maintain a "business as usual" approach, allowing the board to conduct a comprehensive search and the successor to complete a critical M&A deal before taking over.

Qualities of Effective Transitional Leaders

Not every executive is suited for transitional leadership. The role requires a unique blend of skills and temperament.

1. Neutrality and Objectivity

An interim CEO is often an outsider, free from the internal politics and personal agendas that can cloud decision-making. Their impartiality makes them credible in stabilizing tensions.

- **Example:** In a family-owned business grappling with internal feuds between siblings, a neutral interim CEO was brought in to mediate and make decisions based on the company's best interests, not family dynamics.

2. Stability Under Pressure

They must be calm in a crisis, reassuring employees, investors, and customers that the company remains in capable hands, even during turbulent times.

- **Example:** When a public utility company faced a major technical failure that led to widespread outages, the interim CEO became the public face of the company, communicating calmly and transparently with the media and regulators while her team worked to restore service.

3. Clarity and Communication

Transitional leaders excel at communicating transparently, reducing uncertainty, and building trust across all stakeholders.

- **Example:** After a CEO was ousted for ethical violations, the interim leader held a series of all-hands meetings and sent weekly updates, detailing the steps the company was taking to restore integrity and rebuild trust.

4. Strategic Stewardship

They focus not on radical change but on protecting the company's core mission while positioning it for its next phase of leadership. Their job is to hold the fort, not to charge into new territory.

- **Example:** The interim CEO of a well-established nonprofit focused on protecting its core endowment and ensuring grants were distributed on schedule. They avoided launching new, expensive initiatives, instead opting to preserve resources and strategic direction for the permanent leader.

5. Humility

Unlike transformational leaders, interim executives know their role is temporary. Their mission is not personal glory but organisational continuity.

- **Example:** A high-profile executive took on a six-month interim role at a struggling startup. He frequently credited the existing team for their hard work and emphasized that his job was to "get out of the way" as soon as a permanent CEO was found.

6. Experience

Effective transitional executives often have broad experience across industries or turnaround situations, enabling them to step into chaos and quickly create order.

- **Example:** A seasoned veteran of multiple corporate turnarounds was hired as an interim CEO for a manufacturing company facing supply chain collapse. Her previous experience allowed her to diagnose the problem and implement solutions in a matter of weeks, a timeline that would have been impossible for a less-experienced leader.

How Interim Leadership Buys Time During a Transition

One of the most powerful functions of interim leadership is time management. They provide organisations with the time and stability needed to make thoughtful decisions during turbulent transitions.

1. Maintaining Operational Continuity

Employees need to know that payroll will run, projects will continue, and customers will be served. The interim CEO ensures a sense of business-as-usual while restructuring unfolds.

- **Example:** An interim CEO at a software company focused on ensuring all current product roadmaps remained on schedule, reassuring engineering teams that their work was still valued and protected from the leadership change.

2. Stabilizing Stakeholder Confidence
Investors, regulators, and customers watch transitions closely. A transitional leader reassures them that the company remains steady despite the leadership change.

- **Example:** After the abrupt departure of a visionary founder, the new interim CEO held a series of calls with top investors to outline a clear plan for stability and future growth, preventing a stock market overreaction.

3. Enabling a Careful Search for Successors
Boards often make poor decisions when rushed into naming a permanent leader. An interim executive buys time for a thorough evaluation of potential successors, both internal and external.

- **Example:** A Fortune 500 company used an interim leader to conduct a six-month, global search for a new CEO, allowing

48

them to vet dozens of candidates and find the perfect fit rather than simply promoting the most convenient internal option.

4. Protecting the Organisation from Founder Shock

In founder-led businesses, a founder's sudden absence can destabilize the culture. An interim leader helps employees and customers adjust emotionally and structurally.

- **Example:** When the founder of a popular clothing brand stepped down, an interim CEO was appointed to communicate with the company's loyal customer base and employees, reinforcing the brand's original mission and values even without its charismatic creator.

5. Resetting Priorities

Sometimes, a temporary leader can quietly restructure processes, cut unnecessary costs, or resolve internal conflicts, leaving the permanent leader with a healthier organisation.

- **Example:** The interim CEO of a failing media company made the difficult but necessary decision to sell off several non-core assets and downsize the marketing department, leaving the permanent CEO with a leaner, more focused business.

Conclusion: Bridges, Not Monuments

In times of transition, organisations do not need monuments; they need bridges. The interim CEO and transitional executives are those bridges, carrying the company safely across turbulent waters to a future where new leadership can take the reins.

For founders and boards, embracing transitional leadership is not a sign of weakness. It is a mark of wisdom—the understanding that organisations must survive moments of uncertainty with grace, discipline, and continuity. An interim CEO's greatest gift is time. Time for the board to think clearly, for the company to adjust, and for the right successor to emerge.

Chapter 9
BALANCING STABILITY AND CHANGE DURING A TRANSITION

Every leadership transition is a delicate dance between stability and change. Too much stability, and the company stagnates, clinging to the past. Too much change, and the company destabilizes, losing its people, customers, and identity. The art of transitional leadership lies in striking the right balance, keeping the organisation steady while guiding it into a new future.

During these moments, employees feel uncertain, customers worry, investors get anxious, and competitors watch closely. How leaders handle this phase often determines whether the company emerges stronger or weaker.

The Human Element: Managing Employee Morale and Culture

Employees are the heartbeat of any organisation. Leadership changes create ripples of anxiety that can quickly spread if not carefully managed.

1. Acknowledge the Uncertainty

Pretending everything is "business as usual" rarely works. Employees sense change. Acknowledging uncertainty honestly builds trust and reduces the power of rumors.

- **Example:** When a beloved CEO unexpectedly retired, the interim leader held a company-wide town hall, starting with the statement, "I know many of you are feeling uncertain right now, and that's completely understandable. We don't have all the answers yet, but we will be transparent about our process." This simple act of honesty immediately calmed anxieties.

2. Reinforce the Company's Core Values

Culture must act as the anchor. Leaders should reaffirm that while leadership may change, the company's mission and values remain constant. Maintaining rituals, traditions, and symbols of the culture gives employees a sense of continuity.

- **Example:** A food-tech startup known for its collaborative culture and weekly team lunches continued to host these events even during a leadership search. This simple act reinforced the core value of community, showing that the company's spirit was intact despite the transition.

3. Provide Reassurance Without False Promises

Employees don't expect leaders to know everything, but they do expect honesty. Clear communication about what is known and what is still being worked out prevents the spread of rumors and builds a foundation of credibility.

- **Example:** A company facing a merger held a Q&A session where a manager was asked if there would be layoffs. Instead of a vague "we don't foresee any," the honest response was, "We are still assessing roles, but we will communicate a clear plan as soon as it's finalized. Our priority is to be as fair and transparent as possible."

4. Involve Employees in the Transition

Create forums where employees can ask questions and voice concerns. Empowering mid-level managers to act as cultural carriers—those who can interpret the new direction and keep morale steady—is crucial.

- **Example:** A transitional CEO formed a "Future Steering Committee" with employees from various departments. This group was tasked with providing feedback and suggestions for the new leader, making employees feel respected and included in the process.

The Communication Lifeline: Engaging Stakeholders

Communication is the lifeline of successful transitions. Poor communication fuels fear; great communication builds confidence.

1. Employees
Communicate openly and frequently. Silence creates a void that is quickly filled by rumors. Even if the message is "we're still working on this," consistent updates reduce uncertainty.

- **Example:** The interim head of an engineering division sent a short, weekly email to her team outlining her priorities and progress, ensuring they felt informed and included in the ongoing transition.

2. Customers
Reassure clients that the leadership change will not affect the quality of products or services. Personal calls from senior executives to major accounts can calm nerves and prevent competitors from using the transition as a point of attack.

- **Example:** The Chief Revenue Officer of a SaaS company personally called its top 20 clients to introduce the interim CEO, reiterating the company's commitment to service and long-term partnership.

3. Investors
Provide structured updates through board meetings, financial disclosures, and direct communication. Investors need to see that the transition is managed, not chaotic.

- **Example:** Following a CEO's retirement, the board held a special briefing for major shareholders, providing a detailed timeline for the leadership search and outlining a clear strategy for the interim period.

4. Media and Public

Craft a clear and consistent narrative. If the transition is seen as a sign of confusion, competitors and critics will exploit it. If it is framed as a strategic renewal, it strengthens brand trust.

- **Example:** When a CEO was removed for poor performance, the company's press release framed the decision as part of a "strategic and necessary renewal" to drive future growth, controlling the narrative from the start.

Preventing Brain Drain During a Leadership Change

One of the greatest risks during a transition is the loss of key talent. When employees perceive instability, they begin looking for exits, and competitors often seize the opportunity to poach them. To prevent brain drain

1. Identify Key Talent Early

Make a list of mission-critical employees and leaders. Ensure they feel secure and valued during the transition through direct communication and visible support.

- **Example:** The COO of a tech company created a "Top 50" list of essential personnel and had senior leaders personally meet with each person to discuss their future role and value to the organisation.

2. Offer Stability Contracts

Temporary retention bonuses, contracts, or incentives can keep critical talent from leaving during uncertain times.

- **Example:** A private equity firm offered a six-month retention bonus to key executives at a newly acquired company, incentivizing them to stay and help navigate the post-merger integration.

53

3. Involve Them in the Transition

Give high-value employees visibility and a role in shaping the new phase. Inclusion reduces fear and builds commitment.

- **Example:** A CFO-in-waiting was invited to participate in the final interviews for the permanent CEO position, which made him feel respected and invested in the outcome.

4. Reinforce Career Growth Opportunities

Communicate how the transition opens new leadership and growth pathways. When employees see a future for themselves in the organisation, they are less likely to leave.

- **Example:** The interim head of HR held a series of meetings to outline new career ladders and professional development **programme**s, showing employees that the transition was an opportunity for them to advance.

5. Recognize and Appreciate

Leaders should take extra steps to appreciate staff during transitions. Recognition and gratitude build loyalty when financial incentives may not be enough.

- **Example:** The transitional CEO of a consulting firm sent handwritten thank-you notes to team members who worked late to meet a deadline, showing his personal appreciation for their dedication during a stressful time.

The Leadership Balancing Act: Stability and Change

During transitions, leaders must hold two truths at once:
- **Stability:** Protect what is working, preserve culture, and reassure stakeholders.
- **Change:** Embrace renewal, empower new leadership, and adapt to new realities.

It is not an either/or choice. The genius of transitional leadership lies in doing both, reassuring continuity while enabling transformation.

Think of an organisation in transition as a ship at sea. **Stability** is the anchor; it keeps the company from drifting aimlessly during the storm. **Change** is the sail; it catches the wind and moves the company forward. Without the anchor, the ship is lost. Without the sail, the ship is stuck.

Founders and boards that master the balance of stability and change build companies that not only survive transitions but thrive because of them.

Chapter 10
CASE STUDIES OF SUCCESSFUL TRANSITIONAL LEADERSHIP

Stories often teach what theories cannot. While frameworks provide clarity, real-world examples provide conviction. Transitional leadership is not an abstract idea; it is a proven path that has allowed companies across industries, geographies, and ownership structures to survive the exit of their founders and thrive into new generations of leadership. The moments of change, from the carefully planned to the entirely unexpected, are a company's greatest test. The following examples demonstrate that with the right preparation, governance, and mindset, a company can navigate these transitions not just to survive, but to emerge stronger.

In this chapter, we explore three types of case studies: multinational corporations, family-owned businesses, and a personal journey of leadership transitions.

Multinational Corporations That Transitioned Seamlessly

1. Apple – From Steve Jobs to Tim Cook

Few companies were as identified with their founder as Apple was with Steve Jobs. His vision, charisma, and insistence on perfection shaped the culture and products of the company. When Jobs passed away in 2011, many predicted Apple would collapse without him. The company had prepared, however. The board and Jobs himself had identified Tim Cook as his successor years earlier. Cook was not a copy of Jobs, but a different kind of leader: steady, operationally brilliant, and calm under pressure. He focused on supply chain mastery, global expansion, and leveraging Apple's immense financial power, a stark contrast to Jobs's singular focus on product innovation. Under Cook's transitional leadership, Apple grew into the world's most valuable company, proving that an institutionalized vision—

built into the fabric of the company—was the true foundation of success, not just a founder's personality.

- **Lesson:** A strong successor does not need to be a clone of the founder; they need to be a complement. A successful transition requires a different set of skills to take the company to its next stage of growth, supported by strong governance structures.

2. Unilever – Professionalizing Beyond Its Founders

Unilever, founded in the 1920s as a merger of British and Dutch companies, quickly grew into one of the world's largest consumer goods firms. The founders are long gone, but the company thrives because of its deep-rooted governance, professional management, and a strong culture of sustainability and brand stewardship. Unilever's seamless transitions over decades were possible because it invested heavily in leadership pipelines, created a governance framework that deliberately limited founder-dependency, and embedded its core values into its DNA. The company's long-term success is a testament to the fact that institutionalizing leadership is far more durable than relying on the charisma of any single individual.

- **Lesson:** Companies that professionalize early and institutionalize governance structures can thrive across centuries, outliving their founders by design. Building a system that can outlast any single personality is the ultimate act of legacy building.

3. Toyota – Building Leadership as a System

Toyota's success is not tied to a single leader but to "the Toyota Way," a culture of continuous improvement (Kaizen) and respect for people. Leadership transitions at Toyota have been remarkably smooth because leaders are groomed through decades of exposure to the company's systems and culture. The system itself is the leader, and executives are merely the stewards of that system. This approach ensures that the company can transition seamlessly regardless of who holds the CEO title. The focus is on processes, not personalities, creating a predictable and highly resilient organisation.

- **Lesson:** A strong culture and a system-driven leadership model ensure that the company can transition seamlessly regardless of who holds the CEO title. The most successful organisations build a foundation so strong it can weather any leadership storm.

Family-Owned Businesses That Built Beyond the Founder

1. The Tata Group (India)

Founded by Jamsetji Tata in 1868, the Tata Group has survived multiple transitions over 150 years. The conglomerate, which includes companies from steel to software, successfully passed leadership from family members to professional executives, with independent boards ensuring sound governance. The group now operates in over 100 countries, with the Tata legacy—built on principles of social responsibility and ethical conduct—firmly intact. Its ability to professionalize leadership and embrace outside talent is a key reason for its continued relevance and success on the global stage.
- **Lesson:** Family-owned businesses must eventually embrace external leadership and strong governance to survive beyond the second or third generation. A founder's love for the business is a starting point, but professional management is a prerequisite for a lasting legacy.

2. Ford Motor Company (USA)

Henry Ford was one of the most visionary founders in history, but his rigid, unyielding leadership nearly destroyed the company by the 1940s. It was only after his grandson, Henry Ford II, took over and embraced external executives and modern management principles that Ford survived crises and continued as one of the world's largest automakers. The company's journey from a one-man show to a modern corporation is a powerful case study in the necessity of adapting to change and relinquishing control for the greater good of

the institution.
- **Lesson:** Founder stubbornness can doom a company; openness to new leadership and modern governance can save it. The greatest founders are those who build a company capable of outgrowing them.

3. Dangote Group (Africa)

While still founder-led, the Dangote Group, a major African conglomerate, has gradually embraced professional managers, investors, and independent directors. These deliberate steps are preparing the ground for continuity beyond its founder, Aliko Dangote. The move toward institutionalizing governance and involving external stakeholders is positioning the conglomerate to outlive its founder's personal influence and ensure its long-term stability and growth. This proactive approach is a model for family-owned businesses in emerging markets.
- **Lesson:** Even family-owned businesses in emerging markets must build structures today for a tomorrow where the founder is no longer present. The time to plan for a transition is long before it becomes an urgent need.

Lessons from Personal Exits and Leadership Transitions

I have lived through transitions, not just observed them. Over the years, I have founded and led businesses, and I have also exited businesses that continue to thrive today without me.

1. Exiting Without Collapse

One of the greatest lessons I learned as a CEO is that the true test of leadership is not how well the business runs under you, but how well it runs without you. By building robust systems, involving boards in strategic decisions, and empowering successors with genuine autonomy, I was able to exit businesses that did not crumble but continued growing. My role was to create a self-sustaining organism, not a monument to my own leadership.

- **Example:** When I sold my first company, I spent a year working side-by-side with the new leadership to ensure a seamless handover. My focus was not on dictating their every move but on transferring institutional knowledge and empowering them to make their own decisions. The company's subsequent growth, under their leadership, was a testament to the success of that approach.

2. The Pain of Letting Go

Letting go was never easy. As a founder, it feels unnatural to release control. There were moments I feared that successors would ruin what I had built, or that my legacy would be forgotten. But I learned that my role was not to guarantee perfection; it was to guarantee continuity. The pain of letting go was a necessary rite of passage, a final act of stewardship to ensure the organisation's long-term health. The emotional journey from creator to custodian is a difficult but essential one.

- **Example:** After handing over the reins of a company I had built from the ground up, I found myself repeatedly wanting to intervene. It felt like I was watching someone else raise my child. The feeling of separation anxiety was real, but I had to actively force myself to step back and trust the new team. The decision to let them chart their own course was a deliberate act of faith.

3. Surprises of Continuity

In some businesses I left, successors made decisions I would never have made, and yet, those decisions led to growth I had not imagined. This taught me that continuity does not mean uniformity. It means building an organisation strong enough to evolve without losing its essence. The greatest surprise was realizing that my absence was not a void but a space for new ideas and innovations to flourish. The organisation's ability to surprise me in my absence was the ultimate sign of my success as a leader.

- **Example:** Years after leaving a tech company I founded, I watched in awe as the new CEO pivoted the business model in a direction I had considered but never pursued. My initial reaction was skepticism, but the move led to a massive expansion into a new market. I realised then that my departure had created the space for a new vision to take hold, proving that the organisation had a life and purpose beyond my own.

Personal Lesson: You do not truly succeed as a leader until your organisation thrives without you. That is when you move from being a founder to being a legacy builder.

The Power of Transitional Leadership in Every Case

From Apple and Unilever to Tata and Ford, and even in my own journey, the message is clear: transitional leadership is the key to building companies that live beyond their founders.

Some transitions succeed because they are meticulously planned. Others succeed because governance and culture were strong enough to withstand sudden shocks. In every case, the principle holds: companies that prepare for transition thrive; companies that avoid it collapse. The strategic and emotional intelligence required to manage these moments is the ultimate differentiator between a transient success and an enduring institution.

Chapter 11
DESIGNING ORGANISATIONS THAT OUTLIVE THE FOUNDER

Founders are mortal. Institutions are not. If you want your company to live beyond you, it must be designed deliberately to outlast personalities, including your own. That means creating structures, systems, and cultures that endure regardless of who sits in the corner office. The history of business is littered with the corpses of companies that were brilliant personal empires but fragile organisations. Most collapse with their founders because they were designed as extensions of individuals, not as independent, self-sustaining institutions. The key to longevity lies in embedding values into systems, codifying culture and processes, and building innovation engines that keep the organisation relevant long after the founder is gone. This act of designing a timeless entity requires a unique blend of foresight, humility, and a relentless focus on building a legacy that transcends your own time.

Embedding Values into Systems, Not Individuals

At the start, a company's values often live in the founder. Employees learn "how we do things" by observing the founder's behaviour: how they treat customers, how they make decisions, how they handle crises. But this approach is fragile. When the founder leaves, so does the "moral compass" of the company, leading to a void that can quickly be filled with new, and often conflicting, agendas. To outlive the founder, values must be systematized.

1. Document Core Values Clearly

Write down the organisation's non-negotiables: integrity, innovation, customer-first, resilience, or whatever defines your DNA. These are not merely words on a poster; they are the guiding principles for every decision, from hiring to strategy.

- **Example:** Patagonia's core values—"Build the best product, cause no unnecessary harm, use business to protect nature"— are not just a marketing slogan. They are explicitly woven into the company's operational decisions, such as using sustainable materials and donating a percentage of sales to environmental causes.

2. Translate Values into Policies

A value is useless if it's not actionable. If customer-centricity is a core value, embed it into customer service scripts, complaint resolution policies, and performance metrics. If integrity is a value, build compliance structures, audit mechanisms, and whistleblowing systems that protect ethical behaviour.

- **Example:** At Zappos, a company known for its customer service, the value of "delivering WOW through service" is translated into policies that allow customer service representatives to spend as long as they need on a call, without a time limit, to ensure the customer is satisfied.

3. Build Values into Incentives

Reward behaviours that reflect the company's values. Promotion and compensation systems should reinforce not just financial results, but how those results were achieved. This ensures that employees are not rewarded for cutting corners or behaving in ways that contradict the company's identity.

- **Example:** A tech company might give an annual bonus not just for hitting revenue targets, but for demonstrating teamwork and mentorship, reinforcing its core value of "people-first leadership."

4. Values as a Leadership Compass

Leaders who emerge should be judged against the values, not just financial performance. This ensures continuity of spirit even as leadership styles change. A new CEO might have a different approach, but they must adhere to the fundamental principles that define the organisation.

- **Example:** When Satya Nadella took over as CEO of Microsoft, he made a conscious effort to shift the company's culture from a cutthroat, internal-competition model to one based on empathy and collaboration, directly reflecting a new set of values.

Codifying Culture and Processes

Culture is often described as "the way we do things here." For companies that survive transitions, culture is not left to chance—it is codified, documented, and reinforced daily.

1. Codify Culture in Writing

Create a "culture book" or "leadership guide" that defines acceptable behaviour, rituals, and practices. These documents serve as a manual for anyone joining the company, ensuring they understand its identity from day one.

- **Example:** Netflix's famous Culture Deck is a prime example. It explicitly outlines a culture of "freedom and responsibility," setting clear expectations for employees about how they are expected to behave and make decisions.

2. Institutionalize Rituals

Rituals like weekly town halls, recognition ceremonies, or storytelling traditions keep culture alive across generations. These are the touchpoints that connect employees to the company's history and purpose, giving them a sense of continuity during times of change.

- **Example:** Many companies host annual founder's day events or share stories of early challenges and triumphs, reinforcing the core values and mission that got them started.

3. Document Processes Rigorously

From hiring to decision-making to customer support, processes must be mapped and documented. A process-driven organisation doesn't lose its rhythm when leadership changes because the "how" of the business is ingrained in the system, not in a single person's mind.

- **Example:** A manufacturing company's detailed standard operating procedures for the assembly line ensure that production quality remains consistent regardless of who is in charge of the plant.

4. Empower Cultural Ambassadors

Train mid-level managers to act as guardians of culture. Employees must see that the culture is enforced by systems and people at every level, not just the founder. These ambassadors are crucial for translating the founder's vision into everyday reality.

- **Example:** A global retail chain might select and train "cultural champions" in each store to ensure that customer service standards and team values are consistently upheld across all locations.

5. Measure Cultural Health

Conduct regular employee engagement surveys and track how well teams live up to the values in their operations. This provides a data-driven approach to maintaining and improving the company's culture, ensuring it remains a strategic asset.

- **Example:** A company might include questions in its annual survey that directly correlate to its core values, such as "Do you feel empowered to make decisions?" or "Are you encouraged to be innovative?"

Building an Innovation Engine to Keep the Company Relevant

No matter how strong the culture or governance, a company that does not adapt will eventually die. Longevity requires a built-in engine of innovation that allows the company to stay relevant through changing markets, technologies, and customer needs.

1. Dedicated Innovation Teams

Create a division or lab tasked with exploring new markets, products, and technologies. Protect it from short-term profit pressures so it can focus on the long game. This ensures that the company is always looking ahead, not just reacting to the present.

- **Example:** Google's "X" division, a semi-secret lab that works on "moonshot" projects like self-driving cars and drone delivery, operates with a long-term mindset, separate from the company's core business.

2. Encourage Experimentation

Build a culture where failure is treated as a learning opportunity, not a career-ending event. Systems like "innovation budgets" or "hack days" keep creativity alive and ensure that employees feel safe to take risks.

- **Example:** Amazon's famous "two-pizza team" rule encourages small, autonomous teams to experiment with new ideas, allowing for quick testing and iteration without the need for large-scale, bureaucratic approval.

3. Customer Feedback Loops

Companies that endure remain obsessed with customer needs. Build systems to continuously collect, **analyse**, and act on customer feedback. This ensures that the company's evolution is always guided by the needs of its market.

- **Example:** A software company might use a combination of surveys, user testing, and direct feedback from support teams to constantly refine its product based on what customers actually need.

4. Partnerships and Acquisitions

Enduring companies partner with startups or acquire new technologies to stay ahead. This ensures they are not left behind by disruption and can quickly integrate new capabilities into their business.

- **Example:** Facebook's acquisition of Instagram and WhatsApp allowed it to maintain its dominance in social media, integrating new technologies and user bases into its ecosystem.
-
5. Leadership Development as Innovation

Innovation is not just about products. Continuously developing leaders with fresh perspectives ensures the company never grows stale. A commitment to nurturing new talent is a commitment to the company's future.

- **Example:** IBM has reinvented itself multiple times over a century, from hardware to consulting to cloud and AI. What allowed IBM to outlive its founders and early CEOs was not just governance, but a relentless commitment to reinvention and a deep pipeline of leadership.

From Founder-Led to Institution-Built

Designing an organisation that outlives you requires a great deal of humility. It means accepting that your role is not to be the permanent driver, but to be the architect of a system that runs even without you.

- **If values are only in you, they die with you.**
- **If culture is only in your personality, it fades when you exit.**
- **If innovation depends on your ideas, it stops when you leave.**

But if values are embedded in systems, if culture is codified into processes, and if innovation is built into the company's DNA, then your business becomes timeless. These elements transform a company from a personal empire into an institution capable of thriving centuries after the founder is gone. Your legacy as a founder is not what you build while you are present. It is what continues to grow when you are absent.

Chapter 12
FROM FOUNDER TO STATESMAN: REDEFINING YOUR ROLE

For most founders, the company begins as an extension of their identity. They are the builder, the driver, the Firestarter. Every decision flows through them, every success feels personal, and every crisis feels like a wound. This single-minded focus is what brings a company to life, but it is also what can prevent it from truly thriving. For an organisation to live beyond the founder, the founder themselves must evolve. At some point, the role is no longer to operate but to elevate. This transformation, from operator to statesman, is the most difficult but also the most rewarding stage of leadership. It requires the humility to step back, the foresight to build for the future, and the wisdom to know when your greatest contribution is no longer in the details, but in the vision.

Moving from Operator to Visionary

In the early years, survival depends on founders being operators. They wear multiple hats: CEO, marketer, financial officer, and sometimes even janitor. Their fingerprints are on every detail. But as the company matures, this mode of leadership becomes a bottleneck. If the founder remains stuck in operations, the company never outgrows them. The transition requires a profound shift in mindset and behaviour.

1. From Execution to Direction

Instead of doing the work, you guide the work. You move from answering daily emails and approving every project to setting the long-term vision and empowering your team to execute on it.

- **Example:** A founder of a fast-growing software company

realised she was still personally reviewing every line of code. She made a conscious decision to hire a VP of Engineering and shifted her focus to defining the next five years of product strategy, trusting her new leader to handle the day-to-day execution.

2. From Urgency to Strategy

Operators focus on immediate fires and short-term metrics. Visionaries focus on the next decade. The founder's role becomes imagining what the company should be, not handling what the company is.

- **Example:** The founder of a successful retail brand stopped worrying about the quarterly sales report and instead spent his time researching market trends, new technologies, and potential partnerships that would ensure the company's relevance for the next twenty years.

3. From Micromanagement to Empowerment

You stop being the smartest person in the room. You start surrounding yourself with people who are smarter than you in specific areas. Empowered teams create sustainable growth because they can make decisions and innovate without constantly seeking your approval.

- **Example:** A founder who was notoriously hands-on in marketing realised her approach was limiting her team's creativity. She hired a seasoned Chief Marketing Officer, gave them full authority over the budget and strategy, and saw a significant increase in both innovation and campaign effectiveness.

Becoming a Board Chair, Advisor, or Investor

One of the greatest marks of maturity as a founder is accepting that you do not always have to run the company to influence its direction. Many of the world's greatest companies endured because founders evolved into new roles that allowed them to stay connected without being a bottleneck.

1. Board Chair

From the board, the founder can guide strategy, ensure sound governance, and protect the company's core values without interfering in daily operations. This role allows the founder to safeguard the company's mission while giving operational freedom to new leaders.

- **Example:** Bill Gates transitioned from Microsoft CEO to board chair, then advisor, and eventually focused on philanthropy through the Gates Foundation. Microsoft flourished under new leadership while Gates redefined his role as a global statesman, a powerful guardian of the company's long-term vision.

2. Advisor

As an advisor, the founder becomes a mentor to the CEO and executive team. They offer wisdom, networks, and perspective without overshadowing the leadership. This role is a testament to the founder's wisdom and a valuable resource for the new generation of leaders.

- **Example:** Steve Wozniak, co-founder of Apple, has remained an advisor for decades, providing guidance and historical context without being involved in daily operational decisions.

3. Investor

Remaining an investor allows the founder to stay financially connected while emotionally detaching. The company thrives independently, but the founder still shares in its success. This is a crucial step for founders who want to see their creation continue to flourish but need to step away from the emotional and time-intensive aspects of daily leadership.

- **Example:** Many founders of successful startups remain as key investors after selling their companies, using their capital to support new leaders and new ideas within the organisation.

Detaching Ego from Leadership

Perhaps the hardest part of this journey is letting go of ego. For many founders, stepping back feels like irrelevance. If the company thrives without them, they fear it means they were not essential after all. But true legacy requires humility and a profound shift in self-worth.

1. Your Value is Not in Control

Legacy is not proven by how much you control today, but by how much you enable tomorrow. Your greatest value lies in creating a system that can run on its own.

- **Example:** A founder who built a company with a strong leadership pipeline found a sense of fulfillment in watching his protégés succeed, knowing that their victories were a direct result of the foundation he had built.

2. Successors Will Do Things Differently

They will make choices you disagree with. Some will fail, and some will succeed in ways you never imagined. Detaching ego means allowing the company to evolve beyond your personal preferences, a necessary step for an organisation to reach its full potential.

- **Example:** A founder of a media company was initially resistant when the new CEO wanted to move away from print and go entirely digital. She had to learn to trust the new leader's vision, and the move ultimately saved the company from irrelevance.

3. You Are Not the Company

The company must be bigger than your name, your personality, and your presence. Your role is to create an institution, not a monument to yourself.

- **Example:** When Sam Walton, founder of Walmart, died, the company continued its phenomenal growth because he had spent decades building a culture and system that could thrive independently of his personal presence.

4. Celebrate Obsolescence

The ultimate test of leadership is when the company runs better without you. Instead of fearing irrelevance, celebrate it. It means you succeeded in your ultimate mission: creating something that can endure.

- **Example:** A founder of a successful nonprofit was overjoyed when a new generation of leaders came in with fresh ideas and took the organisation to a new level. Her work was done, and her legacy was secure because the mission was in capable hands.

Legacy Over Ego

Transitioning from founder to statesman is the greatest personal transformation in leadership. It demands humility, patience, and trust. But it also brings peace—the peace of knowing that your company is not a prisoner of your presence, but a living institution designed to endure.

The founder who refuses to let go may build a business. But the founder who evolves into a statesman builds a legacy. And legacies, unlike founders, do not die.

Chapter 13
Pitfalls to Avoid in Leadership Transitions

Leadership transitions can make or break an organisation. A well-managed transition strengthens trust, preserves culture, and ensures continuity. A poorly managed one, however, can plunge a company into crisis, erode value, and sometimes even kill the business entirely. The difference often lies not in external threats, but in internal missteps. Many companies fail not because they lack vision or resources, but because they stumble into a set of avoidable mistakes during leadership handovers. Understanding these common pitfalls is the first step toward a successful and seamless transition.

Here are the most common landmines to avoid.

1. Micromanagement and Inability to Let Go

One of the greatest risks during transitions is the founder or outgoing CEO refusing to step aside fully. They often hover over their successors, override their decisions, and insist on controlling details instead of empowering new leadership. This behaviour creates confusion for employees ("Who is really in charge?"), undermines the successor's authority, and prevents the company from moving forward.

- **Example:** In a prominent family-owned business in Asia, the retiring founder refused to relinquish control of key client relationships. He would repeatedly call clients to offer different terms than the new CEO, creating chaos and ultimately causing the loss of a major account. This micromanagement left the successor powerless and a key part of the business in a state of crisis.
- **Lesson:** If you cannot let go, you are not leading a transition; you are blocking it.

2. Poor Board Composition

Boards are supposed to guide and stabilize transitions, but too often, they are filled with friends, loyalists, or family members who lack the independence and objectivity needed for sound decision-making. The result is a board that acts as a rubber stamp for the founder's wishes rather than a true guardian of the company's future.

- **Example:** At a certain point, Uber's governance challenges reflected a weak board that lacked independent oversight. This allowed the founder's dominance to go unchecked, leading to a series of scandals and internal conflicts that destabilized the company until institutional investors intervened and forced a restructuring of the board.
- **Lesson:** A strong, independent board is not optional; it is the backbone of any successful transition.

3. Ignoring Succession Until It's Too Late

Many companies delay succession planning until a crisis hits—a founder's sudden illness, an unexpected resignation, or a death. By then, it's too late. Without a clear plan, power struggles emerge, key talent leaves due to uncertainty, and investors lose confidence, leading to financial instability and sometimes, total collapse.

- **Example:** Pan Am Airways, once the world's most famous airline, collapsed in part because it failed to prepare for leadership changes and industry shifts after its legendary founder, Juan Trippe, left. Without a clear successor and a modern vision, the company quickly lost its way and was unable to adapt to a changing market.
- **Lesson:** Succession planning should start years before a transition, not during a crisis.

4. Over-Personalization of Leadership

When a company's identity is too tied to the founder's

personality, the organisation struggles to re-establish itself when the founder leaves. Employees feel lost without the founder's "style," customers doubt whether the company will remain the same, and successors are pressured to imitate the founder instead of leading authentically.

- **Example:** When a visionary founder of a highly creative advertising agency stepped down, the company's identity was so tied to his personal charisma that clients and employees felt the soul of the business had left with him. The successor, though competent, struggled to gain credibility because he was constantly compared to the founder's larger-than-life personality.
- **Lesson:** Build a company culture that is larger than one person. Otherwise, when the person leaves, so does the company's identity.

5. Choosing Successors Based on Loyalty, Not Competence

Some founders and boards prefer loyalists—family members, close friends, or long-time employees—over the most competent leaders available. While loyalty matters, it cannot replace competence and vision. This **favouritism** can erode credibility, cause talented employees to leave, and lead to a decline in performance.

- **Example:** A founder of a profitable family manufacturing business chose his eldest son as the next CEO, despite the son's lack of relevant industry experience. This decision led to a series of strategic blunders, a loss of market share to more nimble competitors, and the departure of several key executives who felt passed over and demoralized.
- **Lesson:** The best successor may not be the closest, but the most capable.

6. Lack of Communication During Transition

Transitions often fail because leadership assumes silence will "protect stability." In reality, silence creates fear and a vacuum that is quickly filled with rumors and speculation. Employees panic, customers and partners lose trust, and the media fills the vacuum with damaging narratives.

- **Example:** When a founder of a popular tech startup quietly left without a clear public statement, employees and the media immediately began speculating about a scandal or a financial crisis. The company's silence fueled fear and uncertainty, leading to a drop in stock price and a flood of negative press.
- **Lesson:** Communicate early, clearly, and consistently with all stakeholders.

7. Failing to Balance Stability and Change

Some leaders cling so tightly to stability that they block necessary innovation. Others chase aggressive change during transitions and destabilize everything. Both extremes are dangerous. The key is to honor the past while preparing for the future.

- **Example:** A new CEO of a legacy retail brand, in an effort to show he was different from the founder, made radical changes to the company's pricing model and supply chain almost overnight. The changes were so disruptive that they alienated loyal customers and caused a massive loss of revenue, forcing the board to reverse course.
- **Lesson:** Transitions must honor the past while preparing for the future. Balance is key.

8. Neglecting Talent Retention

During leadership changes, high-performing employees often consider leaving. If leaders fail to reassure or incentivize them with clear career paths, engagement, and recognition, a "brain drain" accelerates, taking institutional knowledge and vital skills with it.

- **Example:** After a beloved founder of a design firm announced his retirement, he and the board failed to communicate a clear vision for the future to their top creative talent. Feeling uncertain, many of the firm's best designers were poached by competitors, leaving the company with a significant knowledge gap.
- **Lesson:** Secure key talent during transitions with recognition, engagement, and clear career paths.

9. Treating the Transition as an Event, Not a Process

Many companies see leadership change as a single event: a resignation, an appointment, or a press release. In reality, transitions are processes that unfold over months or even years. Successors need time to gain credibility, employees need time to adjust, and the culture needs time to absorb the change.

- **Example:** A private equity firm announced a new CEO for an acquired company and expected an immediate, seamless handoff. They failed to implement a structured 90-day transition plan that would have allowed the new leader to build relationships and understand the culture, leading to initial missteps and a rocky start.
- **Lesson:** Treat transitions as journeys, not events.

10. Founder Ego

Perhaps the deadliest pitfall is ego. Founders who cannot imagine a company existing without them sabotage transitions by clinging to power, undermining successors, or refusing to accept new directions. This ego-driven behaviour is a poison that can kill a company from the inside out.

- **Example:** An elderly founder of a successful media company,

out of fear of irrelevance, repeatedly blocked his successor's attempts to move the company into digital media. He insisted on clinging to outdated print models, and his ego-driven decisions ultimately drove the company into bankruptcy.
- **Lesson:** Ego kills continuity. Humility builds a legacy.

Avoiding the Landmines of Transition

Transitions are fragile periods, but they do not have to be fatal. By avoiding these common pitfalls—micromanagement, weak boards, a lack of succession planning, poor communication, and ego-driven decisions—companies can move from founder-centric to institution-driven leadership. The ultimate warning is simple: companies die not because leaders leave, but because leaders fail to prepare for leaving.

Chapter 14
Building Institutions, Not Just Companies

Most entrepreneurs start businesses to solve problems, earn profits, or create wealth. This pursuit is a noble one, but wealth creation alone is not enough to secure a lasting legacy. The companies that truly matter, the ones that live for generations and shape the course of history, are not just businesses; they are institutions. Institutions go beyond mere balance sheets and profit margins. They become symbols of trust, pillars of industries, and shapers of societies. They influence culture, create stable employment, set ethical standards, and transform nations. They outlive their founders, becoming timeless entities that continue shaping the world long after the people who started them are gone. The difference between a company and an institution is the difference between making money and making history. It is the profound shift from building something for yourself to building something for generations to come.

Shifting from Wealth to Legacy Creation

At the beginning, wealth is often the primary goal. Founders want financial freedom, comfort for their families, and a return on their immense effort. But if a founder's vision stops at wealth, their company will likely stop with them. Legacy is a different, far-reaching pursuit.

Legacy means:
- Building something that matters beyond profit.
- Creating a system that benefits future generations.
- Designing a company that thrives without your constant presence.

Wealth fades. Legacy endures

This is why visionary founders gradually shift their focus from income statements to impact statements. They ask not only, "How much money did we make this year?" but also, "What difference will this company make 50 years from now?" This shift in mindset transforms a company from a temporary venture into a lasting force for good.

- **Example:** A tech startup founder might choose to sell their company for a billion dollars and retire. They have created wealth, but their impact on the world ends there. A different founder might use that same company to establish a foundation, fund research, or create new industries, ensuring their influence continues for decades. The first created wealth; the second built a legacy.

The Societal Impact of Companies That Live Beyond Founders

When companies survive beyond their founders, the impact is far-reaching and transformative.

1. Communities Thrive

Long-lasting companies provide stable employment across generations. They become anchors for communities, offering not just jobs but also schools, hospitals, and development **programme**s. This stability builds a foundation of prosperity that benefits thousands of families.

- **Example:** For over a century, a manufacturing plant in a small town provided consistent employment, allowing generations of families to buy homes, send their children to college, and build a vibrant community around the company.

2. Industries Mature

Institutions set standards for entire industries. They raise the bar on ethics, innovation, and professionalism. By leading through example, they create an ecosystem of best practices that new entrants must follow.

- **Example:** IBM didn't just build computers; it established the IT industry's standards for corporate ethics, customer service, and professional development, influencing every company that came after it.

3. Nations Advance

Enduring companies contribute to national identity and economic stability. They become symbols of a nation's resilience, innovation, and industrial capacity on the global stage.

- **Example:** The Tata Group in India is not just a collection of companies; it is a symbol of India's industrial and economic rise. Similarly, Toyota became synonymous with Japan's post-war resilience and engineering excellence, helping to shape the nation's global image.

4. Philanthropy Expands

Institutional companies often evolve into forces of social good. Through foundations and corporate social responsibility (CSR) initiatives, they invest in education, healthcare, and poverty alleviation, creating an impact far beyond their commercial operations.

- **Example:** The Tata Group in India funds hundreds of schools and hospitals through the Tata Trusts, impacting millions of lives and contributing to the nation's social infrastructure in a way that no single founder ever could.

Why Lasting Companies Matter For Communities

They provide stability. A lasting company is not just an employer but a lifeline, offering opportunities, skills, and growth to families across decades. This enduring presence creates a sense of security and shared purpose.

- **Example:** A family-owned business that survives for a century provides steady work for multiple generations of employees, becoming a central pillar of the local economy and culture.

For Industries

They set benchmarks. Enduring organisations push innovation, define ethics, and create ecosystems that new entrants rely on. They are the established players that provide a roadmap for others to follow.

- **Example:** When a pharmaceutical company with a hundred-year history develops a new drug, its established reputation for quality and safety sets a high bar for all competitors.

For Nations

They build resilience. Countries with strong institutions have stronger economies, lower unemployment, and greater global credibility. They become the engines of national growth and stability.

- **Example:** Think of how Samsung shaped South Korea, how Siemens influenced Germany, or how Procter & Gamble helped define American consumer goods. These companies are not just businesses; they are national assets.

Case Examples of Institutions That Outlived Founders
Nestlé (founded 1867 by Henri Nestlé)

What began as a small company producing infant cereal is now the world's largest food and beverage company. It has long outlived its founder, and through its commitment to research and nutrition, it continues to shape global food standards.

The Tata Group (founded 1868 by Jamsetji Tata)

Over 150 years later, the Tata Group operates across 100 countries and is synonymous with Indian industrial growth. Its longevity is a testament to its commitment to institutionalizing governance and its core values of integrity and philanthropy, which were codified and maintained for generations.

Unilever (founded 1929 through a merger)

Born from the merger of a British soap maker and a Dutch margarine company, Unilever is now a multinational shaping sustainability practices worldwide. Its ability to professionalize leadership and embed its values allowed it to evolve far beyond its original leaders, becoming a global force in consumer goods.

The Founder's Challenge: Institution vs. Empire

There is a temptation for founders to build empires—businesses centered on personal power, fame, or wealth. Empires die with emperors. Institutions, on the other hand, outlive their builders. The challenge for every founder is to ask:
- Am I building for myself, or for the future?
- Am I chasing short-term wealth, or designing long-term legacy?
- Will my company disappear when I disappear, or will it shape lives for generations?

To build an institution is to think beyond yourself. It is to plant trees whose shade you may never sit under, but which will shelter others for decades to come. It is to accept that the greatest measure of success is not how high your company rises while you are alive, but how strong it stands when you are gone.

Chapter 15
The Future of Transitional Leadership

Leadership has always been about continuity, but the future will demand it in ways we have never seen before. The pace of change is accelerating—industries rise and fall in decades, not centuries. Technologies redefine business models overnight, global markets are more interconnected than ever, and employees increasingly demand meaningful, flexible, and transparent leadership. In this environment, transitional leadership will no longer be a strategy for rare moments of succession; it will become a permanent feature of organisational design. Companies that master it will thrive across generations. Those that ignore it will vanish.

The Impact of AI, Globalisation, and Hybrid Organisations on Transitions

1. Artificial Intelligence (AI)

AI will fundamentally reshape leadership transitions by enabling an unprecedented level of continuity and objectivity.

- **Decision Continuity:** AI systems will increasingly codify leadership knowledge into data-driven systems. Successors will not just inherit manuals; they will gain access to predictive analytics and AI advisors that carry forward institutional wisdom. For example, a new CEO could use an AI platform to **analyse** historical sales data, market trends, and internal performance metrics to understand why a previous product launch succeeded or failed, making their decisions more informed and consistent.

- **Bias Reduction in Succession:** Algorithms, when well-designed, will help identify leadership talent based on objective data like performance metrics, skill sets, and potential for growth, reducing the influence of **favouritism**, nepotism, and unconscious bias in succession planning. A global company could use an AI tool to identify the top 5% of its managers across all departments, regardless of their location or background, for future leadership consideration.

- **AI-Enhanced Governance:** Boards will use AI tools to assess risks, track compliance, and evaluate performance in real time, strengthening oversight during transitions. This allows for a more transparent and data-driven approach to board-level decisions.

2. Globalisation

In a borderless economy, leadership transitions will increasingly affect not just one office but global networks. Successors must be able to operate across cultures, geographies, and regulatory frameworks. Companies must plan for leadership pipelines that are global in scope, not just local.

- **Example:** When a multinational CEO retires, the board must consider candidates not just from headquarters but from key regional offices in Asia, Europe, and Latin America. The new leader's ability to navigate cultural nuances, regulatory differences, and local market dynamics will be as critical as their financial acumen. A misstep in a single market, such as a culturally insensitive press release, can destabilize global trust.

3. Hybrid Organisations

The rise of remote work and hybrid organisations changes how leadership transitions unfold. Successors will need to manage distributed teams across continents, where leadership visibility and trust-building will depend less on physical presence and more on communication, empathy, and digital platforms. Cultural continuity will require new rituals and digital-first traditions to unify global, hybrid teams.

- **Example:** A new CEO of a company with a significant remote workforce can no longer rely on daily walk-arounds to build trust. Instead, they must implement a strategy that includes frequent video town halls, digital "open door" policies via instant messaging, and virtual team-building events to ensure cultural cohesion and communication.

Emerging Models of Governance for Longevity

1. Shared Leadership Models

Instead of a single CEO, companies may increasingly adopt co-CEOs or leadership councils during transitions. This reduces dependency on one person and allows for smoother handovers, as responsibilities are distributed among a team.

- **Example:** A tech company might appoint a co-CEO to focus on product and a co-CEO to focus on operations, allowing for a phased transition as the founder gradually steps back from the day-to-day business.

2. Rotational Leadership

Organisations may rotate leadership roles among executives, ensuring multiple leaders are succession-ready and no one individual becomes indispensable. This creates a deep bench of talent and prevents leadership bottlenecks.

- **Example:** A professional services firm might rotate its office managing partners every three to five years, giving a wider range of partners experience in leadership and preparing them for a potential firm-wide role.

3. Stakeholder Boards

Boards of the future will include not just investors but employees, community representatives, and even AI-driven governance tools, ensuring broader accountability and resilience.

- **Example:** A company focused on sustainability might add a representative from a key environmental non-profit to its board, ensuring its long-term strategy aligns with its stated values.

4. Digital Governance Platforms

Blockchain-based governance systems may ensure transparent, tamper-proof decision-making, reducing political battles during transitions by creating a clear, immutable record of all decisions and votes.

Your Vision for Leadership Beyond Founders in the Next Generation

The next generation of leadership must redefine legacy. Future founders will no longer measure success only by wealth or even innovation, but by whether their companies can stand independently of them. My vision for leadership beyond founders is built on three pillars:

1. Leaders as Architects, Not Operators

The founder's true role will be to design systems, culture, and governance that function without them. Founders must see themselves as architects of continuity, not perpetual operators. This requires a shift in mindset from building a business to building a self-sustaining system.

Example: A founder spends their last year at the company not on daily operations, but on mentoring the next generation of leaders, documenting the company's core principles, and ensuring the board is equipped with the tools to guide the company's future.

2. Organisations as Living Systems

Companies must evolve from rigid hierarchies into adaptive systems, capable of learning, innovating, and regenerating themselves across generations. A living system can respond to change and heal from setbacks without a single point of failure.

- **Example:** A global conglomerate creates an internal venture capital fund that allows employees to pitch new business ideas. The most promising ideas are spun off into new units, ensuring the company continuously regenerates itself from within.

3. Legacy as Institutional Impact

The new measure of legacy will not be how much money a founder made, but how many generations the company serves, how many industries it shapes, and how many communities it uplifts.

- **Example:** A founder's legacy is not measured by the IPO value but by the fact that the company they built provided stable, meaningful employment for a century, shaped an entire industry's ethical standards, and funded a foundation that lifted thousands out of poverty.

The Future Belongs to Transitions

The world is moving too fast for static leadership. The companies that thrive will be those that embrace transitional leadership as a continuous discipline, embedding it into governance, culture, and strategy. The founder of the future is not a ruler but a statesman, not a controller but an architect. And the organisations of the future will not be companies that die with their leaders; they will be institutions that live beyond them.

Chapter 16

Conclusion: Living Beyond You

Every founder begins with a dream. Some dream of solving problems, others of financial freedom. Some want to change industries, and a few want to change the world. Regardless of the dream, every founder must eventually face the same question: Will my company die with me, or will it live beyond me?

This book has explored that question in depth, examining the principles, structures, and leadership models that enable companies to outlast their founders. The journey has revealed a single, powerful truth: true leadership is not about being indispensable, but about creating continuity. It is a transition from building a personal empire to architecting a lasting institution.

Summary of Principles

Across these chapters, we have laid out a blueprint for transitional leadership—a set of timeless principles that form the architecture of an immortal company.

- **Founders must let go to grow.**

    The journey from operator to statesman is defined by the humility to release control. As we saw in "From Founder to Statesman," clinging to micromanagement creates a bottleneck that stifles a company's growth, while a founder's release of control empowers the next generation to take the organisation further than ever imagined.

- **Governance is the backbone of continuity.**

    The chapter on "Pitfalls to Avoid" demonstrated how a weak or biased board can sabotage a transition. Strong, independent boards and clear governance frameworks are not optional;

they are the essential infrastructure that ensures a company can survive the departure of its founder.

- **Succession is not an event but a process.**

We learned that ignoring succession planning until a crisis hits is one of the most common pitfalls in leadership transitions. Identifying and grooming leaders must begin years before the founder is ready to step aside, creating a seamless and stable handoff.

- **Culture must be codified, not personified.**

An over-personalization of leadership ties a company's identity to its founder's personality. The principles outlined in this book emphasize the need to build a culture that is bigger than one person, one that is embedded in values, rituals, and systems that can be carried forward by future leaders.

- **Institutions matter more than empires.**

As we explored in "Building Institutions, Not Just Companies," empires centered on personal power die with their emperors. Institutions, in contrast, live on to serve communities, mature industries, and advance nations for generations, proving that a company's true value lies in its impact, not just its profit.

- **The founder must evolve into a statesman.**

This is the ultimate leadership transformation. It is the journey from being in the trenches to becoming an architect of legacy, from managing day-to-day operations to safeguarding the long-term vision. The statesman's legacy is measured not by how much they controlled, but by how well they enabled others.

- **The future belongs to leaders who design for continuity.**

    The final chapter demonstrated how forces like AI, **globalisation**, and hybrid work are making transitional leadership a permanent feature of organisational design. The leaders of tomorrow will not just inherit titles; they will inherit AI-enhanced decision systems and global, distributed teams, requiring them to be architects of continuity in both physical and digital spaces.

Personal Reflections on the Journey

    These words are not born of theory alone. They have been forged through the lived experience of founding and exiting companies. I have felt the bittersweet tension of letting go and the fear of wondering if a successor will undo your work. But I have also known the profound pride of seeing a team take a vision further than I ever imagined possible.

    Through it all, I have learned that leadership is not measured by how much power you hold, but by how well your organisation thrives when you release it. The greatest leaders are not those who build companies that shine in their lifetime, but those who build institutions that endure for lifetimes. This book is the roadmap I wish I had in my earliest ventures—a reminder that the real test of leadership is not success today, but continuity tomorrow.

A Call to Action for Leaders

    As you close this book, I leave you with a challenge:
    Do not build a company that dies with you. Do not build an empire that collapses when its emperor is gone. Do not build wealth that evaporates when your hands can no longer hold it.
    Instead, build an institution.
    Build systems that outlive your personality. Build leaders who carry forward your vision in ways you never imagined. Build governance that protects your company from ego, **favouritism**, and

fragility. Build a culture that future generations will inherit with pride.

Because in the end, leadership is not about you. Leadership is about the people, the communities, the industries, and the nations that your company will serve long after you are gone.

To live beyond yourself, you must build beyond yourself. And that is the true calling of transitional leadership.

www.ingramcontent.com/pod-product-compliance
Lightning Source LLC
Chambersburg PA
CBHW071723210326
41597CB00017B/2568